Engaging God's Word

Daniel

Engage Bible Studies

Tools That Transform

Engage Bible Studies

an imprint of

 COMMUNITY BIBLE STUDY

Engaging God's Word: Daniel, 2nd Edition
Copyright © 2014 by Community Bible Study. All rights reserved.
ISBN 978-1-62194-022-7

Published by Community Bible Study
790 Stout Road
Colorado Springs, CO 80921-3802
1-800-826-4181
www.communitybiblestudy.org

Unless otherwise noted, all Scripture quotations are from the *Holy Bible, English Standard Version*® (ESV®). Copyright © 2001 by Crossway, a publishing ministry of Good News Publishers. Used by permission. All rights reserved. ESV Text Edition: 2011.

Scriptures quotations marked (NIV) are from the *Holy Bible, New International Version*®, NIV®. Copyright © 1973, 1978, 1984, 2011 by Biblica, Inc.® Used by permission. All rights reserved worldwide.

Printed in the United States of America.

Contents

Introduction

Welcome to the life-changing adventure of engaging with God's Word! Whether this is the first time you've opened a Bible or you've studied the Scriptures all your life, good things are in store for you. Studying the Bible is unlike any other kind of study you have ever done. That's because the Word of God is *"living and active"* (Hebrews 4:12) and transcends time and cultures. The earth and heavens as we know them will one day pass away, but God's Word never will (Mark 13:31). It's as relevant to your life today as it was to the people who wrote it down centuries ago. And the fact that God's Word is living and active means that reading God's Word is always meant to be a personal experience. God's Word is not just dead words on a page—it is page after page of living, powerful words—so get ready, because the time you spend studying the Bible in this *Engaging God's Word* course will be life-transforming!

Why Study the Bible?

Some Christians read the Bible because they know they're supposed to. It's a good thing to do, and God expects it. And all that's true! However, there are many additional reasons to study God's Word. Here are just some of them.

We get to know God through His Word. Our God is a relational God who knows us and wants us to know Him. The Scriptures, which He authored, reveal much about Him: how He thinks and feels, what His purposes are, what He thinks about us, how He views the world He made, what He has planned for the future. The Bible shows us God's many attributes—His kindness, goodness, justice, love, faithfulness, mercy, compassion, creativity, redemption, sovereignty, and so on. As we get to know Him through His Word, we come to love and trust Him.

God speaks to us through His Word. One of the primary ways God speaks to us is through His written Word. Don't be surprised if, as you read the Bible, certain parts nearly jump off the page at you, almost as if they'd been written with you in mind. God is the Author of this incredible book, so that's not just possible, it's likely! Whether it is to find comfort, warning, correction, teaching, or guidance, always approach God's Word with your spiritual ears open (Isaiah 55:3) because God, your loving heavenly Father, has things He wants to say to you.

God's Word brings life. Just about everyone wants to learn the secret to "the good life." And the good news is, that secret is found in God's Word. Don't think of the Bible as a bunch of rules. Viewing it with that mindset is a distortion. God gave us His Word because as our Creator and the Creator of the universe, He alone knows how life was meant to work. He knows that love makes us happier than hate, that generosity brings more joy than greed, and that integrity allows us to rest more peacefully at night than deception does. God's ways are not always "easiest" but they are the way to life. As the Psalmist says, *"If Your law had not been my delight, I would have perished in my affliction. I will never forget Your precepts, for by them You have given me life"* (Psalm 119:92-93).

God's Word offers stability in an unstable world. Truth is an ever-changing negotiable for many people in our culture today. But building your life on constantly changing "truth" is like building your house on shifting sand. God's Word, like God Himself, never changes. What He says was true yesterday, is true today, and will still be true a billion years from now. Jesus said, *"Everyone then who hears these words of Mine and does them will be like a wise man who built his house on the rock"* (Matthew 7:24).

God's Word helps us to pray effectively. When we read God's Word and get to know what He is really like, we understand better how to pray. God answers prayers that are according to His will. We discover His will by reading the Bible. First John 5:14-15 tells us that *"this is the confidence that we have toward Him, that if we ask anything according to His will He hears us. And if we know that He hears us in whatever we ask, we know that we have the requests that we have asked of Him."*

How to Get the Most out of *Engaging God's Word*

Each *Engaging God's Word* study contains key elements that have been carefully designed to help you get the most out of your time in God's Word. Slightly modified for your study-at-home success, this approach is very similar to the tried-and-proven Bible study method that Community Bible Study has used with thousands of men, women, and children across the United States and around the world for nearly 40 years. There are some basic things you can expect to find in each course in this series.

❖ Lesson 1 provides an overview of the Bible book (or books) you will study and questions to help you focus, anticipate, and pray about what you will be learning.

❖ Every lesson contains questions to answer on your own, commentary that reviews and clarifies the passage, and three special sections called "Apply what you have learned," "Think about" and "Personalize this lesson."

❖ Some lessons contain memory verse suggestions.

Whether you plan to use *Engaging God's Word* on your own or with a group, here are some suggestions that will help you enjoy and receive the most benefit from your study.

Spread out each lesson over several days. Your *Engaging God's Word* lessons were designed to take a week to complete. Spreading out your study rather than doing it all at once allows time for the things God is teaching you to sink in and for you to practice applying them.

Pray each time you read God's Word. The Bible is a book unlike any other because God Himself inspired it. The same Spirit who inspired the human authors who wrote it will help you to understand and apply it if you ask Him to. So make it a practice to ask Him to make His Word come alive to you every time you read it.

Read the whole passage covered in the lesson. Before plunging into the questions, take time to read the specific chapter or verses that will be covered in that lesson. Doing this will give you important context for the whole lesson. Reading the Bible in context is an important principle in interpreting it accurately.

Begin learning the memory verse. Learning Scripture by heart requires discipline, but the rewards far outweigh the effort. Memorizing a verse allows you to recall it whenever you need it—for personal encouragement and direction, or to share with someone else. Consider writing the verse on a sticky note or index card that you can post where you will see it often or carry with you to review during the day. Reading and re-reading the verse often—out loud when possible—is a simple way to commit it to memory.

Re-read the passage for each section of questions. Each lesson is divided into sections so that you study one small part of Scripture at a time. Before attempting to answer the questions, review the verses that the questions will cover.

Answer the questions without consulting the Commentary or other reference materials. There is great joy in having the Holy Spirit teach you God's Word on your own, without the help of outside resources. Don't cheat yourself of the delight of discovery by reading the Commentary prematurely. Wait until after you've completed the lesson.

Repeat the process for all the question sections.

Prayerfully consider the "Apply what you have learned," marked with the ✎ push pin symbol. The vision of Community Bible Study is not to just gain knowledge about the Bible, but to be transformed by it. For this reason, each set of questions closes with a section that encourages you to apply what you are learning. Usually this section involves action—something for you to do. As you practice these suggestions, your life will change.

Read the Commentary. *Engaging God's Word* commentaries are written by theologians whose goal is to help you understand the context of what you are studying as it relates to the rest of Scripture, God's character, and what the passage means for your life. Of necessity, the commentaries include the author's interpretations. While interesting and helpful, keep in mind that the Commentary is simply one person's understanding of what these passages mean. Other godly men and women have views that are also worth considering.

Pause to contemplate each "Think about" section, marked with the notepad symbol. These features, embedded in the Commentary, offer a place to pause and consider some of the principles being brought out by the text. They provide excellent ideas to journal about or to discuss with other believers, especially those doing the study with you.

Jot down insights or prayer points from the "Personalize this lesson" marked with the ☑ check box symbol. While the "Apply what you have learned" section focuses on doing, the "Personalize this lesson" section focuses on becoming. Spiritual transformation is not just about doing right things and refraining from doing wrong things—it is about changing from the inside out. To be transformed means letting God change our hearts so that our attitudes, emotions, desires, reactions, and goals are increasingly like Jesus'. Often this section will discuss something that you cannot do in your own strength—so your response will usually be something to pray about. Remember that becoming more Christ-like is not just a matter of trying harder—it requires God's empowerment.

Lesson 1

God Is in Control

Is God approachable, personal, and intimately involved in the details of our daily lives? Or is He a God beyond our galaxy, wrapped up in the Cosmic Control Center of the universe? In the book of Daniel, we see that He is both! He works in the intimate details of Daniel's life, equipping, encouraging, and empowering Him to live well under terribly difficult circumstances. But He also works in the grand scheme of history, unveiling some mysteries while keeping others veiled, but all the while reassuring us that He is in control and that no matter how bad things around us seem, we need never to worry because He is working it all together for good.

Some of the themes you'll encounter in Daniel include:

❖ God is sovereign over kings and kingdoms, and history, past, present, and future.

❖ God is establishing a kingdom that will never pass away.

❖ God enables His people to live godly lives in ungodly environments.

❖ God empowers His people to make a positive influence in their culture.

❖ God humbles the proud and lifts up the humble.

❖ A spiritual battle lies behind every physical battle.

❖ Prayer is the believer's resource in the midst of conflict and trouble.

1. Do you typically think of God in terms of His intimate involvement in your life? Or do you more often think of Him in terms of His role as Lord of the universe? How could thinking of Him in both biblically accurate ways benefit you?

    _____

    _____

    _____

2. Which of the themes listed above are you most familiar with? Which one offers the biggest stretch for you? Why?

    _____

    _____

    _____

3. Read the list of themes in Daniel again. Which one seems especially important for your spiritual growth right now? Why?

    _____

    _____

    _____

If you are doing this study with a group, take time to pray for one another about your answers to these three questions. Ask God to reveal truth to you as you study about this and, even more importantly, to make you more like Jesus as a result. If you are studying by yourself, write your prayer in the blank space below.

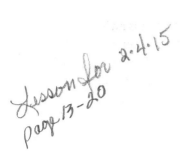

Lesson for 2·4·15
page 13-20

Lesson 1 Commentary

God Is in Control

The book of Daniel is set in a land and time far removed from our own, yet it could hardly be more relevant to us. Does it ever seem like you are living in a culture that doesn't understand you or the things that you value? Have you ever struggled to speak up for truth and reason among people who do not seem interested in truth or reason? If so, then the book of Daniel promises to be a meaningful study for you.

The book of Daniel tells of a young Jew, Daniel, who was taken to Babylon when the Jewish nation went into captivity. While living in pagan Babylon, Daniel firmly maintained his faith in God, experienced miraculous rescue from persecution, and received prophetic visions. Though Daniel was a faithful Jew and wrote primarily to Jews, his book reached out to the Gentile world as much as any book in the Old Testament.

Daniel was probably just a teenager when he was taken as a captive from Jerusalem to Babylon, more than 500 miles away. He was removed from everything familiar—his family, friends, culture, and way of worship. But Daniel was not removed from God. God remained close to him. In fact, it was in this extremely hostile setting that Daniel's relationship with God became stronger. From the time we meet Daniel in 605 BC until the end of his story 68 years later, we see Daniel's wisdom, grace, faith, and integrity. Daniel is one of the few Bible characters about whom no sin is mentioned. He is truly a role model for how to live in troubled times.

Think about thriving in a culture that does not honor God, care about people, or acknowledge truth. Although he lived more than 2,500 years ago, Daniel's story has a contemporary feel. The

challenges Daniel faced are similar to the ones we face
today—although ours are not usually quite as intense! But
God never failed Daniel, and Daniel never failed Him.
Daniel was faithful to God. The book of Daniel shows that
even in an ungodly culture, it is possible to start out
strong—and finish strong.

Historical Background

When Daniel wrote his prophecies, the Jewish nation was going through
one of the most violent upheavals in its history. Centuries earlier, Joshua
had led Israel into the Promised Land, where it became an independent
nation with its own leaders on its own soil.

But Israel rebelled against God. God had repeatedly warned His people
about the consequences of their rebellion. His warning to Judah's King
Hezekiah was very clear (Isaiah 39:6-7). But the people of Judah refused
to repent, and the disaster God had warned them about came to pass.
God handed the nation over to judgment and eventually into captivity
under the Babylonians and their renowned leader, Nebuchadnezzar.

Nebuchadnezzar laid siege to Jerusalem. The Babylonian army burned
the temple, tore down the city's walls, and killed or deported the people
who still lived there. The city was ruined. God's people were defeated.

The experience of captivity was shattering. The Israelites were suddenly
without a land, a temple, a priesthood, and a holy city—and most of
them were forcibly resettled to thoroughly pagan and Gentile Babylon,
hundreds of miles away. To encourage them and to tell of God's
purposes—not only for them but for the pagan nations as well—the
Lord raised up Daniel to write this book. The book of Daniel was
probably composed near the end of Daniel's life.

Think about the times you have felt as though
everything was falling apart and God was no longer
in control. If you feel that way right now, you can
understand how Israel must have felt. Daniel was
written to reassure us that, from God's standpoint,

everything is on schedule, fitting into His great plan, and we don't need to panic. Daniel also encourages us to be unwavering and firm in our faith in a world that increasingly rejects God and the teachings of Scripture.

Structure of the Book

The first half of Daniel is narrative, giving easy-to-understand third-person accounts of the challenges and victories Daniel and his three friends, Shadrach, Meshach, and Abednego, faced while in exile. We see God rescuing His servants from terrifying threats—a capricious king, a fiery furnace, a den of lions. We see Him overruling human plans in order to accomplish His own greater purposes.

The second half of Daniel is different. Chapters 7–12 detail a series of visions Daniel had, full of strange images and symbols that Daniel himself did not understand. They are apocalyptic in nature, relating to the end of the world. He was overwhelmed by all he saw, and did not know what it meant.

In this study, we will not attempt to sort out the meaning of Daniel's prophetic visions. God has intentionally left some things temporarily hidden in mystery. Instead, we will focus on the important themes of Daniel taken from the accounts and principles that apply to all believers.

As you study Daniel, enjoy the interaction between God and Daniel, a man whom He *"greatly loved"* (9:23; 10:19). Notice Daniel's character, heart, and actions. He can teach you how to live out your faith. Also notice God's character, His heart, and His actions. As you get to know God better, you will find your faith growing.

Personalize this lesson.

✓ In times of turmoil and trial, a person's true character usually becomes apparent. The book of Daniel reveals Daniel and his Jewish friends refusing to surrender to the pagan ways of Babylon. They courageously stood their ground even though their lives were repeatedly threatened. The source of their courage is their trust in God as a living, caring, all-powerful Being who would not desert them. The trials you face may not be as life-threatening as Daniel and his friends' were, but each one still represents an opportunity to demonstrate your confidence in God and the reality of Christ living in you. If trials cause something less than faith and goodness to spill out of you, ask God to change you from the inside out. Ask Him to build your faith in Him as you study this book so that you, too, can demonstrate godly character in the face of difficulty.

pray 1st

1:19-18

Lesson 2

Daniel and His Friends Are Deported
Daniel 1

❖ Daniel 1:1-2—Babylon Invades Judah

1. What happened to Judah in the third year Jehoiakim was king?
   Nebuchadnezzer, King of Babylon, came to Jerusalem & besieged it. The Lord delivered Jehoiakim into his hand.

2. According to verse 2, who was responsible for Judah's defeat?
   The Lord

3. Why would God allow His chosen people to be conquered?
   (See also Deuteronomy 28:15, 25, 36; Ezekiel 39:23-24.)
   They did not obey God.

4. What did Nebuchadnezzar do with the sacred temple articles he carries off? What motive(s) might he have for doing this?
   He took them back to Babylonia & the Temple of his gods.

❖ Daniel 1:3-7—Learning Babylonian Ways

5. From this passage, how would you describe Daniel and his friends who were deported with him?
   The same as Daniel.

6. Why do you think the king selected people with qualities such as the ones Daniel and his friends possessed?

_____

_____

7. The king gave Daniel and his friends new names. What else did he do to indoctrinate them to Babylonian culture?

_____

_____

8. How might the requirements Nebuchadnezzar placed on the young men have made it hard for them to remain faithful to God?

_____

_____

_____

start 2:11

❖ Daniel 1:8—Refusing the King's Food

9. What did Daniel decide not to do?

Not to defile himself with the royal food & wine.

10. We do not know for certain why Daniel refused to eat the king's food. But Scripture gives us some possible reasons. Look up each of the verses that follow and write a possible reason Daniel had this conviction about the king's food. *ox, sheep, goat, deer, antelope, mountain sheep.*

a. Deuteronomy 14:3-20 *No detestable thing. any animal w/ a split hoof/divided in 2 & chews the cud.*

b. Proverbs 31:4-7 *Not for kings to drink, nor rulers to crave beer.*

c. Acts 15:20, 29 *Food polluted by idols, meat of strangled animals & from blood.*

11. How did Daniel handle his concern? *Daniel said to the guard* *"Test them, for 10 days. Just veg. & water. At the end of the 10 days they looked better than the others"*

12. Have you ever had a conviction that went against the culture around you? What did you do?

    Terry was to have healthy food. The others wouldn't eat it. We fixed 2 meals.

❖ Daniel 1:9-16—Daniel's Request *Eunuchs = Chief official under the king & queen.*

13. How did the chief of the eunuchs respond to Daniel's request?

    He was afraid of the king who assigned the food & drink. He didn't want them to look worse than the others their age.

14. What part did God have in helping Daniel stand firm?

    God caused the official to show favor & sympathy to Daniel

15. From these verses, what do you learn from Daniel's experience that could help you in situations where your Christian values are tested? *Trust in the Lord* *God knows all & will make sure we do not compromise our Christian values.*

❖ Daniel 1:17-20—God Blesses Daniel and Friends

16. What did God give to the four youths? *Knowledge & understanding of all kinds of literature & learning*

17. What did God also give to Daniel? *God gave visions and dreams of all kinds.*

18. Where do you think the magicians and enchanters got their wisdom and understanding? Why was Daniel's wisdom better than theirs?

Daniel's was better because it came from God.

19. What is one way you would like to be more like Daniel? Ask God to develop this trait in your life.

Singlemindedness in God.

Life moves in & takes precidence over God. (Cost of meds, Xtns. worry) about self.

start 2-18-15

 Apply what you have learned. At this point, Daniel and his friends were simply giving up the king's food. Later in their lives, they would face greater challenges. Their response to the king's food was preparation for these larger tests. It is not clear that eating Nebuchadnezzar's food was an actual sin. However, Daniel and his friends chose to view it as a matter of personal integrity. So they took their stand and refused the king's food. In this way, they grew stronger for the bigger tests that would come their way later. Is there a questionable area in your life where you are doing something that isn't necessarily "wrong," but it isn't necessarily "right," either? Ask God, and write down anything you think He may be revealing. Consider using this questionable area as an opportunity to develop your faith and integrity. Quietly and respectfully take a stand. It will probably cost you something—offer it to God as a sacrifice of love.

Daniel and His Friends Are Deported
Daniel 1

By 605 BC, Nebuchadnezzar had conquered Israel; he did not destroy Jerusalem or the temple until about 20 years later—586 BC. In the meantime, he made Israel a colony and allowed it to rule under his authority. However, to strengthen his own kingdom and to weaken conquered Israel, he took a number of the young Jewish nobility to Babylon, where he could train them in Babylonian ways and put them to work in his kingdom. Among those taken were Daniel and several of his peers.

Repeatedly, the book of Daniel emphasizes that God is in control; God is running things. The Lord is both loving and just, yet *"He does not leave the guilty unpunished"* (Exodus 34:7, NIV). If we, like the Israelites, continue in our sinning, we should not be surprised if God allows us to experience painful consequences of sin. But we should know that even then He loves us, and He is waiting for us to repent so He can restore us. That's the good news of the gospel (Acts 3:19-20).

The Young Men Go Into Captivity

The youths Nebuchadnezzar picked were some of Israel's most outstanding young leaders. They were young men *"without blemish, of good appearance and skillful in all wisdom, endowed with knowledge, understanding learning, and competent to stand in the king's palace"* (1:4). They were to learn the language and literature of Babylon, complete three years of training, and then enter the king's service. They were to serve in the government of one of the most powerful rulers of all time. In addition, they were to have their food and lodging supplied by the royal court. However, there was a catch: in order to enjoy these privileges, they had to cooperate with Babylon's pagan leaders.

First, Nebuchadnezzar changed their names. Daniel, Hananiah, Mishael, and Azariah became Belteshazzar, Shadrach, Meshach, and Abednego (1:6-7). In the ancient world names often described characteristics of the persons named. Daniel meant *God is my judge.* Hananiah meant *the LORD shows grace.* Mishael meant *who is what God is?* Azariah meant *the LORD helps.* Nebuchadnezzar would hardly want his leading officials to have names that declared the greatness of Israel's God! So instead they were given new names tied to Babylonian gods. For example, Belteshazzar probably meant *Bel* (a pagan god) *protect his life,* while Abednego meant *servant of Nebo* (another pagan god).

Think how difficult this would have been for these young men. How would you like to have your name changed so that its very meaning announces that you honor something you don't believe? What should they do?

The Young Men Refuse the King's Food

The young men decided to draw a line. They would accept the names, the training, and the positions that might result, but they would refuse the king's rich food. Daniel 1:8 describes eating this food as defiling themselves. How could food defile them? We cannot be certain. Most Bible scholars interpret this in the light of Jewish food laws, which prohibited eating certain foods, such as pork and certain kinds of seafood. Eating the king's food probably violated these laws. In addition, pagan priests probably had presented these foods to pagan gods in a pagan temple.

Think about refusing to compromise your faith. Like the Jewish young men in Babylon, we have to think and pray through areas where we are pressured to conform to our culture. There are places where we must draw lines. God—and only God—deserves first place in our lives. Read 1 John 2:15 and Matthew 6:24. We must ask ourselves "Who is first in my life? Where does my ultimate loyalty and faith rest?"

What resulted from Daniel and his friends following this diet? At the end of the 10 days, they looked healthier than all the others. God had sustained them and honored their faith. God not only protected them, but eventually exalted them to high positions in the Babylonian kingdom, where He could use them to protect the Israelites.

These four young men of faith established a pattern that enabled them to succeed despite Nebuchadnezzar's cruelty. They were going to trust God, confident that He was powerful enough to take care of them. They chose to please God, not man.

Think about why many of us cave in to temptation. Sometimes the reason is not a lack of integrity. Sometimes it's because of our insecurity and fear. We may doubt that God has our best interests at heart or worry that he won't be there for us, so we need to do whatever we can to protect ourselves. In desperate situations like these, we are prone to compromise. But it seems that these young men really trusted God, with all their being. They believed His promises enough to stake their lives on them. Ask God to help you act according to your confidence in Him and His Word and not in reaction to your fears.

Personalize this lesson.

Go back through Daniel 1 and notice how many times the phrase *"God gave"* or *"the Lord gave"* appear. According to these verses, what kinds of things did God give? What does that suggest God is doing with regard to the details of your life? Think about areas of your life that tend to make you anxious. Write one or two of them below. Next to each one, write a truth about God that corresponds to the situation. For example, if an area that makes you anxious is finances, next to that you might write, "My God will supply all my needs." After you have made your list, ask God to help you to trust Him in each of these areas of your life.

- finances
- living arrangements

Nebuchadnezzar's Dream
Daniel 2:1-23

❖ Daniel 2:1-6—The King's Troubling Dreams

1. What upsetting symptoms did Nebuchadnezzar experience as a young king?

   _____

   _____

   _____

2. What did Nebuchadnezzar demand of his wise men?

   _____

   _____

3. What made the king's demand especially unfair?

   _____

   _____

   _____

   _____

4. What did Nebuchadnezzar promise if the wise men succeeded?

   _____

   _____

5. What did he threaten if they failed?

   _____

   _____

❖ Daniel 2:6-11—The King Distrusts His Wise Men

6. What do you learn from verse 9 that reveals that the king does not fully trust his wise men?

   _____

   _____

   _____

7. How do the Chaldeans respond to Nebuchadnezzar's demand?

   _____

   _____

8. Who do you think shows greater wisdom and humility in this passage, the wise men, or the king? Explain your answer.

   The wise men. They knew there was
   someone wiser than they were

   _____

❖ Daniel 2:12-16—Daniel's Life Is Threatened

9. Daniel was not present when the king made his demands of the wise men. Why, then, did the king threaten Daniel and his companions with death?

   _____

   _____

   _____

10. What words describe the manner in which Daniel responded to Arioch when he came to kill Daniel and his companions? What do these words suggest about Daniel's attitude?

    Wisdom & Tact

    _____

    _____

    _____

11. According to verse 15, what did Daniel ask Arioch?

    [handwritten]

12. What favor did Daniel request of the king?

    time

❖ Daniel 2:17-18—Daniel Asks God for Help

13. What did Daniel ask his friends to do?

    Pray to God

14. When you encounter a crisis, do you have friends you can ask to pray for you? If so, how does knowing that others are praying with you help you?

❖ Daniel 2:19-23—Daniel Thanks God

15. How did God answer the prayer of Daniel and his friends?

    God's timing is perfect

16. When God answers one of your desperate prayers, how do you typically respond?

17. From his prayer of thanks, list some of the different things Daniel praised God for.

_____

_____

_____

18. From your answer to the previous question, which of these aspects of God do you appreciate most right now? Why?

_____

_____

_____

Apply what you have learned. Daniel understood the value of having prayer partners. When his life was threatened, he sought prayer support from his friends. Do you have any friends you can ask to pray with you and for you when important needs arise? Are you that kind of friend for others? This week, make an intentional effort to ask at least one other person to pray with or for you about something. What was that experience like for you?

Start
March 4, 2015

Nebuchadnezzar's Dream
Daniel 2:1-23

Daniel is the picture of calm in crisis. Nebuchadnezzar made impossible demands of his wise men. When they could not do what he demanded, he impulsively ordered their execution. As part of the king's staff of wise men, Daniel and his young friends faced this same threat. However, Daniel responded with wisdom, faith, and dignity. And God rewarded Daniel's trust by giving him the interpretation to Nebuchadnezzar's dream. Nothing is too hard for God. He did not abandon Daniel in crisis, and He will not abandon you.

Nebuchadnezzar's Dream and Threat

"The second year of reign of Nebuchadnezzar" (2:1) probably was 604 BC. That same year he attacked Jerusalem, taking Daniel and his friends captive. The next year of his reign probably was troubled, and Nebuchadnezzar had a disturbing dream. He was ready to execute all his wise men, including Daniel, because no one could tell him the content or interpretation of the dream.

Dreams carried a special significance for ancient people. Kings' dreams were seen as communications from the gods about the state and its future. Nebuchadnezzar's response to his dream was to call in Babylon's intellectual elite to interpret it.

The king demanded that his wise men not only interpret his dream, but also tell him what the actual dream was. When they could not do what he asked, Nebuchadnezzar reacted in fear. His reaction revealed his cruel and selfish character. If the wise men did not do as he demanded, he threatened that they would be *"torn limb from limb and* [their] *houses shall be laid in ruins"* (2:5). The wise men, the best and the smartest in Babylon, could not meet the king's impossible demand—so they were about to lose their lives. In this atmosphere of fear and distrust in the royal court, Daniel and his friends had to learn to cope and survive.

Think about how impossible circumstances can serve to point us to God. Nebuchadnezzar demanded that his wise men do what only God could do. However, even though they were pagans, they were wise and humble enough to see their limitations. They recognized that no human being could do what the king had asked, only *"the gods, whose dwelling is not with flesh."* Without knowing it, these men pointed Nebuchadnezzar to God. When people find themselves in desperate circumstances, they often make impossible demands from those around them. When this happens to us, we would be wise to point them to God, who alone is capable of doing the impossible.

Although Babylon's wise men were admired and respected in the ancient world, this passage exposes their weakness and limitations. They could not do what the mentally unstable, tyrannical king demanded. So Nebuchadnezzar ordered the execution of all the wise men of Babylon (2:12- 13). This included not just the smaller group called in to interpret his dream, but all the other wise men, as well as those in training, including Daniel and his three friends.

The urgent situation provided the opportunity for God to show His power and majesty to idol-worshiping Nebuchadnezzar. God would help Daniel and his friends, even though they were young, conquered foreigners, to do what the king's wise men could not.

Daniel Seeks God

Daniel spoke with *"prudence and discretion"* to the commander of the king's guard, Arioch. When Arioch showed up on Daniel's doorstep, ready to execute him according to Nebuchadnezzar's command, Daniel responded without anger or panic. Instead, he calmly asked Arioch to appeal to the king for time to ask God for an interpretation.

Like the king's wise men, Daniel knew that he could not do what the king had asked. However, he knew that his God could. Before going home to pray, however, he sought the support of his friends. Together they pleaded to God for mercy, that they might receive the interpretation of the king's dream and have their lives spared (2:18).

In a vision in the night, God did indeed reveal to Daniel the content and interpretation of Nebuchadnezzar's dream.

Daniel's Prayer of Thanks

We can imagine how excited Daniel must have been when God revealed Nebuchadnezzar's dream to him. But he did not rush off to tell the king. He did not even go immediately to report to his friends this wonderful answer to prayer. Instead, he paused to thank God and worship Him. Some commentators have called Daniel's beautiful prayer "Daniel's Psalm."

Daniel praised God who has wisdom and power, who *"changes times and seasons"* and *"removes kings and sets up kings"* (2:21). His prayer reflects the dream's interpretation, which will be explained later in the chapter. The interpretation emphasizes that God controls history.

The *"times and seasons"* describe the character of different time periods (times of war, times of peace, and so on) and the length of the periods. God controls it all—what happens, when it will happen, and how long it will last.

This assurance of God's sovereignty encourages all believers, but it especially would have encouraged the dispossessed Israelites under mighty Babylon's rule. In their position of subjugation and captivity, the Israelites might have understandably been tempted to doubt God's power. They might have wondered if God had deserted them. But Daniel's prayer of praise reminds them—and us—of God's faithfulness and power.

Think about how praise and worship are just as important as making our needs and desires known to God. Prayer is more than just asking God for help and provision. Prayer is also worship and thanksgiving. Even when facing life-and-death pressure from an angry and impulsive despot, Daniel did not hurry from God's presence. God answered his prayer, so Daniel paused to thank Him and worship Him. His thanks revealed his dependence on God just as much as his petition did.

Personalize this lesson.

☑ How was Daniel able to remain calm and steady even under threat of death? Probably Daniel's inner strength came through his study of God's Word and reflection on God's character. We know from Daniel 9 that Daniel knew the Scriptures. We also know that the Psalms were sung as a regular part of temple worship in Jerusalem before Daniel went into captivity. Perhaps Daniel remembered Psalm 46 when Arioch came to execute him. Psalm 46 starts out, *"God is our refuge and strength, a very present help in trouble. Therefore we will not fear though the earth gives way ... "*

Do you long to be stable and secure when crises show up at your doorstep? If so, consider choosing a Psalm to make your "own." Besides Psalm 46, other possibilities include Psalm 23, 27, or 91. Write down some of your favorite verses from the Psalm. Pray them back to God each day this week and ask Him to use their truth to make you strong and steady in the core of your being.

Arioch = Commander of the kings guard.
Daniel spoke with wisdom & tact & asked the
King for time.
Daniel asked his 3 friends to pray to the heavens
for mercy

The Dream and Its Interpretation
Daniel 2:24-49

❖ **Daniel 2:24-30—Daniel Goes before the King**

1. What request did Daniel make of Arioch?

   Do not execute the wise men of Babylon. Take me to the king and I will interpret his dream for him.

2. In view of the fact that Nebuchadnezzar's wise men were pagan practitioners of the occult, why do you think Daniel spoke up to save their lives?

   To save innocent lives, Daniel knew the request was futile. and to show them about God.

3. What did the king ask Daniel before allowing him to give the interpretation? Why was this so important to the king?

   _____

   _____

4. What does Daniel's response to the king say about Daniel? (2:27-30)

   Only a God in heaven can reveal mysteries.

5. What do you learn about God from what Daniel said in 2:27-30?

   He was telling Nebuchadnezzar that only He knew.

❖ Daniel 2:31-35—Daniel Reveals the King's Dream

6. What stands out to you from Daniel's description of the image Nebuchadnezzar saw in his dream?

   It was like an idol

7. What effect would a dream like Nebuchadnezzar's have on you? How would you feel? What might you be thinking or wondering?

   I wouldn't understand it

8. What ultimately happened to the image?

   Crumbled

9. Describe the stone in Nebuchadnezzar's dream.

10. Who does the Bible often refer to as a "*Rock*" or a "*Stone*"? (See Isaiah 26:4; Acts 4:10-12; 1 Peter 2:4, 6-8).

❖ Daniel 2:36-45—The Image, Part 1

11. How did Daniel describe each part of the image Nebuchadnezzar saw in his dream, the material it was made of, and what it represented? (Also refer to 2:32-35.)

12. Moving from head to toe, what do you notice about the strength of the image and the empires it represents?

_____

_____

❖ Daniel Daniel 2:36-45—The Image, Part 2

start 3/11

13. From 2:37-38, how did Daniel describe Nebuchadnezzar, his power, and his influence? *King of kings, He has given you dominion, power & might & glory. He has placed mankind & beasts of the field & birds of the air. The ruler over all. The head of gold.*

14. How does knowing that God gives rulers their authority encourage you, challenge you, or prompt you to pray? *I do not know what God wants. Nor do I know the far reaching goals of our leaders. Therefore pray for God's will to be done.*

15. What is true about the kingdom the God of heaven will set up? How is it different from the other kingdoms in Nebuchadnezzar's dream? *It will never be destroyed. God will rule. It will not be oppressive. It will crush all other kingdoms. This is the meaning of the rock.*

❖ Daniel 2:46-49—Nebuchadnezzar Responds

16. Describe Nebuchadnezzar's response to Daniel, after Daniel had interpreted his dream. *He fell prostrate before Daniel. ordered an offering & incense be presented to him. Surely your god is the God of gods, Lord of kings a revealer of mysteries.*

17. Why do you think a great ruler like Nebuchadnezzar would respond this way to a lowly exile? *The Holy Spirit was with him?*

_____

18. What does Nebuchadnezzar say about God? Do you think he is
a true believer? Why or why not?

He is the God of gods, Lord of king

19. What did Nebuchadnezzar do for Daniel? *He promoted Daniel
to ruler over the whole provence of Babylon,
Daniel also asked that Nebuchadnezzer
promote his 3 friends as well.*

Love your enemies

Apply what you have learned. We can be
quite sure that Daniel would not have chosen to live
as an exile in Babylon. We can also be pretty certain
that he would have preferred not to live in a thoroughly
pagan culture so far from the home and people he loved.
However, Daniel understood that God could use him
anywhere. He did not allow undesirable circumstances to
hinder him from being who God called him to be and doing
what God called him to do. *He listened*

Consider your personal circumstances. Which ones seem
undesirable to you? Have you considered your situation a
hindrance to serving God? Ask God to help you see your
circumstances the way He sees them. How can you fully be
who He has called you to be right now? How can you serve
Him in the situation He has placed you in? After you have
talked to Him, write down some thoughts about it.

---

*I don't know
Be an example of His love*

start 3-18-15

The Dream and Its Interpretation
Daniel 2:24-49

Because Daniel sought God for help interpreting Nebuchadnezzar's dream, he was able to spare not only his own life, but the lives of his three friends and of all the wise men in Babylon. God revealed the dream's meaning to Daniel. The message of the king's dream was more far-reaching than anyone could have imagined.

Daniel Goes before Nebuchadnezzar

Daniel's compassion and love for all.

Daniel asked the captain of the king's guard, Arioch, not to kill the king's wise men. He promised that if Arioch would take him to Nebuchadnezzar, he would give Nebuchadnezzar the interpretation to his dream. *He's total confidence in the Lord.*

---

§ **Think about** blessing your enemies. Daniel probably would not have considered Nebuchadnezzar's magicians, astrologers, and wise men as friends. They did not worship the true and living God. They were superstitious people who, if they had any power at all, got it from the powers of darkness. Daniel had no reason to care about sparing their lives. In fact, it might have been easier for him if they had been put to death. But Daniel was a righteous man. He spoke up for these people who had been unjustly sentenced to death. In this way, he fulfilled the words Jesus spoke centuries later: "*Love your enemies, do good to those who hate you.*" (See Luke 6:27, 32-33, 35.)

The beheadings (We seem to care more for the Christians than all the others as well.)

God gave Daniel ability to do what Nebuchadnezzar's men could not. As a result, the king's wise men were exposed as powerless. Instead of taking credit for himself, Daniel gave credit to "*God in heaven.*" It was God, not Daniel, who chose to inform Nebuchadnezzar of the future.

Think about how witchcraft, magic, and other occult practices are as ineffective in solving life's problems now as they were in Nebuchadnezzar's time. Besides being ineffective, they are also deceptive and dangerous. Spiritual practices that are not grounded in God and His Word open the door to Satan and his demons. Deuteronomy 18:10-12 directly condemns such action. If you have put your trust in Jesus, the Spirit of the living God lives inside you (Romans 8:9). Your body is His temple, and "*What fellowship has light with darkness?*" and "*What agreement has the temple of God with idols?*" (2 Corinthians 6:14, 16). The Spirit of God is greater than the powers of darkness (1 John 4:4). If we belong to Jesus, occult practices should have no place in our lives. Our trust is in God alone.

Daniel Interprets the Dream

Daniel explained the interpretation God had given him. He said that Nebuchadnezzar represented "*the head of gold*" (2:37-38). Though the king was the head of gold, his reign would not last forever. Eventually Nebuchadnezzar's kingdom would give way to another kingdom. This kingdom would be inferior to Nebuchadnezzar's, symbolized by the silver part of the image. Following this, a third kingdom, pictured by the bronze middle and thighs, would arise "*which shall rule over all the earth*" (2:39).

But Daniel devoted most of his attention to a fourth kingdom. This kingdom was represented by the iron legs and feet of iron and clay. The fourth kingdom would "*break and crush*" the nations (Daniel 2:40). Yet like iron mixed with clay, it would be "*partly strong and partly brittle*" (2:42). "*As you saw the iron mixed with soft clay, so they will mix with one another ... but they will not hold together, just as iron does not mix with clay*" (2:43).

Daniel made it clear that God sovereignly caused these kingdoms to rise and fall. God had established Nebuchadnezzar and his magnificent Babylonian kingdom. He would cause another kingdom to succeed it, followed by a third kingdom that would rule over that whole area of the world. A fourth kingdom would then arise, powerful enough to crush its foes, yet strangely brittle and weak. God would then raise up an eternal kingdom that will utterly destroy all the others. This kingdom is His own kingdom that will never pass away.

Most Bible scholars believe that the empires represented by the king's dream-image were the Medo-Persian, Greek, and Roman empires. In 539 BC, Babylon fell to the Medo-Persian kingdom—the chest and arms of silver. Persia was inferior to Babylon in that its rulers never possessed the absolute unchallenged authority of Nebuchadnezzar. In 330 BC, Persia fell to Alexander the Great and Greece, the belly and thighs of bronze. This kingdom covered much of the then-known world. It stretched from southern Europe across the Middle East to India. It also spread the Greek language and culture across the world. This is why the New Testament was later written in Greek.

We must not miss the point: God controls the nations. As Proverbs 21:1 says, "*The king's heart is a stream of water in the hand of the LORD. He turns it wherever He will.*" The most powerful rulers have authority only because God gives it to them. We can rest in this truth today.

Nebuchadnezzar's Response

Daniel's interpretation stunned Nebuchadnezzar. He fell on his face before Daniel. The great king realized that Daniel was an agent of the most high God. Accordingly, Nebuchadnezzar proclaimed, "*Truly, your God is God of gods and Lord of kings, and a revealer of mysteries*" (2:47). He promoted Daniel to "*ruler over the whole province of Babylon*" (2:48). At Daniel's request, the king promoted his three friends as well. This royal act preserved their lives and helped to keep Israel alive during the years of captivity.

Personalize this lesson.

✓ God's principle is clear: *"Those who honor Me I will honor, but those who despise Me will be lightly esteemed"* (1 Samuel 2:30). God accomplishes something else through fiery trials. The three friends went into the furnace tied up by *"some of the mighty men of* [the] *army"* (3:20). Yet verse 25 specifically states that the three men were *"unbound"* as they walked around in the fire. Determining to honor God regardless of circumstances frees us. We are no longer bound by fear and can move through our trials with peaceful hearts because we trust that our good and loving God is in control. What circumstance has you bound by anxiety and fear? Can you give that situation to God and let Him handle it for you? Ask Him to increase your ability to trust Him and not to be afraid.

The Salvation of the family.

Lesson 5

The Fiery Furnace
Daniel 3

Memorize God's Word: Acts 5:29.

❖ Daniel 3:1-7—The King Sets up a Golden Image

1. How would you describe the image Nebuchadnezzar set up on the plain of Dura?

   A golden mass. Worth money. Something one might see on a tour of a museum.

2. What do you think motivated the king to erect such an image?

   Arrogance? Self

3. What did Nebuchadnezzar command the crowd at the ceremony to do? What was the penalty if they refused?

   Whenever they heard the sound of music, they were to fall down & worship it.

4. How would the king's command have presented a moral dilemma for the exiles from Israel? (See Exodus 20:3-6.)

   Daniel & his friends were believers in God only.

5. If you had been one of the exiles, how do you think you would have responded to the king's command? Explain your answer.

I would pray that I would refuse to worship this false idol.

start april 1

❖ Daniel 3:8-15—Daniel's Friends Are Accused

6. What did *"certain Chaldeans"* accuse Shadrach, Meshach, and Abednego of?

Not obeying Nebucadnezzer.

7. What do you think motivated the Chaldeans to make such malicious accusations? List all the possibilities you can think of.

Fear of being thrown into the fiery furnace. They may not have liked them in charge of what Nebucadnezzer had assigned to them.

8. Daniel 3:13 records that King Nebuchadnezzar was furious with rage. Why do you think he was so angry?

Because he was trustful of them & they were not with the idols.

9. How would you explain the disparity between what the king says in 2:47 and what he says and does in 3:15?

Jealous of our God

❖ Daniel 3:16-18—Daniel's Friends Take a Stand

10. How do Shadrach, Meshach, and Abednego respond to the king's commands and threats?

The God we serve will save us. We will not serve your gods.

11. Think back to what you have studied in Daniel so far. What had God already done to show His care for Shadrach, Meshach, and Abednego?

_____

_____

12. Did Shadrach, Meshach, and Abednego know for certain that God would save them this time? What does this say about their faith?

Yes, they were with God.

_____

13. Have you ever taken a bold or risky stand for God? What was that like for you?

Not always good. It made me feel alone, even tho I knew God was w/ me.

start 4.8.15

❖ Daniel 3:19-27—The Miraculous Deliverance

14. How did Nebuchadnezar respond after Shadrach, Meshach, and Abednego told him they would not bow to his image?

He became angry and had the 3 thrown in the fiery furnace.

15. What details from 3:19-23 suggest Nebuchadnezzar was not acting rationally?

His attitude changed when the 3 refused to worship Nebuchadnezzers gods.

16. What did Nebuchadnezzar see when he looked into the furnace?

The 3 fully clothed but he saw 4 men in the fire.

17. Who do you think the fourth man in the furnace was? For help, consider Daniel 3:25, 28, and Isaiah 43:2-3.

A son of the gods - The Lord your God the Holy one of Israel your Savior.

❖ Daniel 3:28-30—The King Praises God

18. What did the king say and do that showed his respect for God?

   Praise be to the God of Sh., Me. & Abednego. who has sent. His angel. He promoted them in the province of Babylon.

19. What did Nebuchadnezzar say and do that showed his respect for Shadrach, Meshach, and Abednego?

   Promoted them

20. How did God use this event to protect the Israelites in Babylon?

   He promoted them in the province of Babylon.

21. Hebrews 11 is often called the "Faith Hall of Fame" chapter Some scholars think Hebrews 11:34 refers to Shadrach, Meshach, and Abednego. Read Hebrews 11:1-3, 6. How do these young men demonstrate the faith this passage describes?

   By faith we understand that the universe was formed by God's command. So what is seen was not visable.

Apply what you have learned Shadrach, Meshach, and Abednego served God unconditionally. When the king threatened to kill them, they refused to serve false gods or worship an idol (see 3:18). They made it clear that they did not worship God so that He would do something for them in return. These men served Him simply because He was worthy of being served. Think about the expectations you have when you serve God and others. Do you offer your service unconditionally? Or do you hope to get something back? What would it be like to serve with no expectation of personal benefit? Try it this week.

The Fiery Furnace
Daniel 3

Faith in Trial

Nebuchadnezzar's respect for God seemed to vary according to his circumstances. In chapter two he experienced God's power and gave Him praise. But in chapter 3, he returned to idolatry and to making rash and cruel decisions. In this lesson we see the humble faith and courage of God's men, Shadrach, Meshach, and Abednego. The threat of death had no power over them—they would not blaspheme their God! What attitude enabled them to stand firm in such tough circumstances? Simply this: they loved and feared God. They trusted Him to do what He knew was best. *Unconditional*

Nebuchadnezzar Builds a Golden Image

Nebuchadnezzar's dream in chapter 2 should have caused him to humble himself before God. Instead, he became obsessed by the dream's portrayal of his empire as the golden head on the image. His arrogant response is to construct a huge golden image and command the people to bow down to it. He planned an emotionally stirring ceremony and required leaders from all over his empire to attend. Perhaps he hoped that by demanding this public show of loyalty he might be able to unify his vast empire.

The image was about 90 feet high and 90 feet wide. It was built on the *"plain of Dura,"* perhaps a suburb of the city of Babylon. This location would have made the idol visible for quite a distance. It was probably gold-plated rather than solid gold. All the people were to prostrate themselves in worship whenever they heard the musical instruments play. Verse 6 notes that, according to the king's decree, whoever did not fall down and worship would immediately be thrown into a burning furnace.

Think about how temporary the effects of spiritual experience can be. The king had just had an incredible experience with God. God had miraculously revealed to him the mystery of his amazing dream. In awe, Nebuchadnezzar had bowed down and proclaimed Daniel's God to be the "*God of gods and Lord of kings*" (2:47). But the king quickly forgot God and led the entire empire into idolatry. Spiritual experience is not the same as faith. Spiritual experiences come and go, but true faith endures.

The Men Refuse to Bow Down

Shadrach, Meshach, and Abednego were under incredible pressure to conform. But they did not waver. They knew the Ten Commandments. The Lord had said, "*You shall have no other gods before Me*" (Exodus 20:3). So the three men quietly refused to participate. While the Babylonian crowd bowed at the sound of the music, Shadrach, Meshach, and Abednego remained standing. The three men's enemies noticed their quiet defiance. Daniel 3:8-12 says they accused the Jews maliciously: "*These men, O king, pay no attention to you; they do not serve your gods or worship the golden image that you have set up.*"

Nebuchadnezzar Reacts

Enraged, Nebuchadnezzar summoned Shadrach, Meshach, and Abednego. If they would not worship the image as he had ordered he would send them to the blazing furnace. The king's threats did not intimidate the three men. They confidently replied, "*If this be so, our God whom we serve is able to deliver us from the burning fiery furnace, and He will deliver us out of your hand, O king. But if not, be it known to you, O king, that we will not serve your gods or worship the golden image that you have set up*" (3:16-18).

Their response to the king is one of the greatest declarations of faith in the whole Bible. They knew that if God existed—and they were certain He did—then He could rescue them from a mere mortal like Nebuchadnezzar and the lifeless images he worshiped. We are called to have the same faith. We need to be willing to stand on, and perhaps even to die for, that same truth: The God of the Bible does exist. He is still all-powerful. He is "*the same yesterday and today and forever*" (Hebrews 13:8).

Think about faith. Shadrach, Meshach, and Abednego's faith was not based on the belief that God would deliver them from death. Their faith was based on God Himself. Whether He chose to save them—or not—they would trust Him and no one else. Faith wouldn't be faith if it always guaranteed the outcome we hope for. By definition, faith means trusting God regardless of personal benefit or cost. *Unconditional*

God Performs an Astounding Miracle

Infuriated by the young men's words, the king became completely irrational. Apparently he could not believe that anyone would have a higher loyalty than to him. He ordered the furnace to be heated *"seven times more than it was usually heated"* (3:19). Nebuchadnezzar commanded the young men to be bound and thrown into the furnace, fully clothed. The king's command was so urgent that *"the fire killed those men who took up Shadrach, Meshach and Abednego"* (3:22).

However, God did choose to intervene. Instead of being instantly consumed, the men walked around the inside the furnace, untouched by the fire. Furthermore, although the king had cast three men in, he now saw *"four men unbound, walking in the midst of the fire, and they are not hurt; and the appearance of the fourth is like a son of the gods"* (Daniel 3:25). Who was this fourth man? It could be an angel. Or it could be a pre-incarnate appearance of Jesus Christ. Either way, God rescued His servants.

Astonished, Nebuchadnezzar went as close as he could to the blazing furnace. He shouted, *"Shadrach, Meshach and Abednego, servants of the Most High God, come out, and come here!"* (3:26). So they walked out of the furnace (3:27). Everyone gathered around and *"the hair of their heads was not singed, their cloaks were not harmed, and no smell of fire had come upon them."*

They had been thrown in heavily clothed and bound, but nothing had burned but the ropes! Earlier, Nebuchadnezzar had asked, *"Who is the god who will deliver you from my hands?"* Now he and all his officials knew the answer. Nebuchadnezzar praised the God of Shadrach, Meshach, and Abednego (Daniel 3:28-29). He decreed that anyone who spoke against the God of Shadrach, Meshach, and Abednego would be punished because, *"there is no other god who is able to rescue in this way."* (3:29).

Personalize this lesson.

Daniel's three friends faced a huge, life-threatening trial. But God had prepared them for it. From their first days in Babylon, God had given them opportunities to grow their faith. They had refused to defile themselves with the king's food and God had protected them. When the king threatened to kill all his wise men, God spared their lives by giving Daniel the interpretation to Nebuchadnezzar's dream. So when this big trial came, they were ready. Have you ever faced a huge test of faith? How did God prepare you for it in advance?

as far back as I can remember there have been unbelievers. My Mother instilled in me that God is everywhere.
Yes, doubt came into my life but not unbelief. Many questions so I aligned myself with believers. I now am proving to myself by reading the whole truth.

Start 4:29

Lesson 6

God Humbles Nebuchadnezzar
Daniel 4

❖ **Daniel 4:1-3—Nebuchadnezzar Praises God**

1. It seems that King Nebuchadnezzar wrote the account recorded in this chapter. According to 4:1-3, to whom did he write, and about whom?

   To all the world, he told them about the Most high God.

2. How did Nebuchadnezzar refer to God, and what did he say about Him?

   Most high God, His kingdom is eternal, His dominion endures from generation to generation.

3. As you read Nebuchadnezzar's words about God, what encourages you most?

   That he was not a believer and now has changed

❖ **Daniel 4:4-18—The King's Alarming Dream**

4. How did Nebuchadnezzar describe his life at the beginning of his story (4:4-9)?

   At home in his palace content and prosperous. He then had a dream that made him afraid.

5. What words did Nebuchadnezzar use to describe his emotional response to the dream he had?

   It made him afraid. The visions & images terrified him.

6. In your own words, describe the tree Nebuchadnezzar saw in his dream. What made it so valuable?

   The tree was very large & strong, a beautiful tree with fruit. It was seen by everyone and would feed everyone. (It represented God.)

7. In view of his wise men's earlier failure to interpret his dream, why do you suppose Nebuchadnezzar summons them first, rather than Daniel, for help with his dream in chapter 4?

8. What did the "*watcher*" say would happen to the man who was represented by the tree? (4:15b-16)?

❖ Daniel 4:19-27—Daniel Interprets the Dream

9. Daniel hesitated before sharing the interpretation of the dream. In fact, Nebuchadnezzar had to coax him to respond. Why do you think Daniel hesitated?

10. According to Daniel's interpretation of the dream, whom did the tree represent? What was going to happen to him?

11. What did the stump represent? How does it symbolize hope?

_____

_____

12. How did Daniel say the experience would end for the king?

_____

_____

_____

❖ Daniel 4:28-33—The King's Dream Comes True

13. What was Nebuchadnezzar doing 12 months later? What was his attitude at the time?

_____

_____

14. Why do you think God allowed a full year to pass before He brought about the things He had warned Nebuchadnezzar about in his dream? (See 2 Peter 3:9.)

_____

_____

15. Nebuchadnezzar's terrible dream was fulfilled exactly as Daniel predicted. Do you think Nebuchadnezzar could have done anything to prevent this outcome? Explain your answer.

_____

_____

_____

❖ Daniel 4:34-37—God Restores Nebuchadnezzar

16. What did Nebuchadnezzar do, according to 4:34? What do you think his action means?

_____

_____

17. What happened after Nebuchadnezzar lifted his eyes to heaven?

_____

_____

18. How did Nebuchadnezzar's attitude change as a result of his time of humbling? (Compare 4:30 with 4:34-35.)

_____

_____

_____

19. What do you learn about God from the way He dealt with Nebuchadnezzar in this chapter?

_____

_____

_____

Apply what you have learned.
Nebuchadnezzar was very proud. He seemed to think the universe revolved around him. His thoughts usually focused on himself. Such self-centeredness is always dangerous. Do you have any self-centered tendencies? Here's one way to find out. Choose a day this week when you will know you will a lot of interaction with others. From the time you wake up until the time you go to bed, try not to use any personal pronouns ("I," "Me," "My," "Myself," "Mine"). Notice how often you are to refer to yourself. Were you surprised?

start
May 13

Lesson 6 Commentary

God Humbles Nebuchadnezzar
Daniel 4

God had to bring Nebuchadnezzar low in order to help him recognize the source of his greatness. But it doesn't have to be that way. We can be diligent to do what the king did not do: We can humbly ask the Lord if there are areas of pride in our lives that we need to repent of. Then we can listen and respond to Him. We can avoid a lot of heartache if we make a habit of humbly seeking God this way.

Nebuchadnezzar's Dream of the Great Tree

Nebuchadnezzar began his testimony by addressing "*all peoples, nations and languages that dwell in all the earth*" (4:1). The king intended to share his story with the whole world—not just a few people. Nebuchadnezzar praised God for the great signs and wonders He had performed. Perhaps he was thinking of miracles such as saving the three Jews in the blazing furnace. He acknowledged that God's kingdom is eternal and enduring.

Then the king related the details of a fearful dream: "*I, Nebuchadnezzar, was at ease in my house and prospering in my palace. I saw a dream that made me afraid. As I lay in bed the fancies and the visions of my head alarmed me*" (4:4-5). The king turned again to his wise men and advisers. This time, as before, they could not provide a satisfactory interpretation.

Finally, the king sought out Daniel and revealed the dream to him. He saw a tree that was tall and grew strong (4:10-11). It had beautiful leaves and abundant fruit. It sheltered animals and provided a home for birds (4:12). The tree was huge, flourishing, and prosperous.

But then came the dream became troubling. Nebuchadnezzar heard a "*watcher, a holy one*" (probably an angel) command the tree to be chopped down. The watcher commanded the tree to be stripped of its leaves and branches. Only a stump was to remain. The person represented by the tree was to *"be wet with the dew of heaven."* He would live among *"the beasts in the grass of the earth."* Instead of a man's mind, he would have the mind of a beast. This would happen for *"seven periods of time."*

Daniel Interprets the Dream

Nebuchadnezzar's dream distressed Daniel. He hesitated to tell the king its meaning. But Nebuchadnezzar urged Daniel not to allow his alarm to keep him from revealing the interpretation. He wanted an explanation, even if it had negative implications. So Daniel reluctantly agreed to interpret it.

 Think about how speaking the truth requires love and courage. No one wants to be the bearer of bad news. But Daniel lovingly did this for the king. He was less concerned with being "nice" or "polite" than he was with speaking the truth—graciously—that could, if Nebuchadnezzar chose to listen, spare the king much heartache and humiliation. Daniel was a good example for all of us. He modeled how to speak the truth in love (see Ephesians 4:15).

Daniel explained to Nebuchadnezzar that the flourishing and fruitful tree that provided food and shelter represented him. The king was flattered. But Daniel's interpretation also made it clear that the cutting down of the tree represented the king himself being humbled (4:25): *"You shall be driven from among men, ... You shall be made to eat grass like an ox, ... till you know that the Most High rules the kingdom of men and gives it to whom He will."*

God Humbles the Arrogant King

Daniel respectfully advised Nebuchadnezzar to change his ways. He urged the king to stop sinning and start practicing righteousness. He encouraged him to show mercy to the oppressed. Daniel explained that if the king made these changes, *"there may perhaps be a lengthening of your prosperity"* (4:26).

Think about God's patience with sinners. Nebuchadnezzar was harsh, proud, and cruelly oppressive. God would have been completely just if He had struck the king dead immediately. However, God chose to be patient with him. He showed the king his sin and urged him to repent. We see that God's goal was not to punish, but to bring Nebuchadnezzar to repentance. The king is an example of someone who presumed *"on the riches of His kindness and forbearance and patience, not knowing that God's kindness [was] meant to lead [him] to repentance"* (Romans 2:4).

One day, while walking on the palace roof, Nebuchadnezzar gazed at his beautiful dwelling, with the city around him, and boasted: *"Is not this great Babylon, which I have built by my mighty power as a royal residence and for the glory of my majesty?"* (4:30). As the king boasted, God struck him down: *"He was driven away from people and ate grass like cattle. His body was drenched with the dew of heaven until his hair grew like the feathers of an eagle and his nails like the claws of a bird"* (4:33). Nebuchadnezzar literally went insane for seven long years (the *"seven periods of time"* in 4:23). It is difficult to imagine a more humiliating experience.

Nebuchadnezzar Recovers

Finally, the king recovered (4:34-35). God healed him when he raised his eyes to heaven. And when his reason returned to him, he responded by blessing God. His description of God's sovereign control of the world is one of the greatest biblical passages on this subject. He acknowledged that God rules over all. Nobody has authority over God. No one can tell Him what to do—not even a great ruler like Nebuchadnezzar.

Such a confession of God's greatness would be significant coming from anyone. But coming from a king who had more absolute power over more human beings than any other person on earth at that time makes it even more remarkable. Besides restoring Nebuchadnezzar's sanity, God also restored his kingdom and permitted him to reassume his throne. Nebuchadnezzar concluded his praise by acknowledging the true King and professing: *"Now I, Nebuchadnezzar, praise and extol and honor the King of heaven, for all His works are right and His ways are just; and those who walk in pride He is able to humble"* (4:37).

Personalize this lesson.

☑ The Israelites were captives in Babylon. They were despised foreigners living far from home. They lived under the frightening rule of an unpredictable and irrational pagan king. There was nothing about their situation that would have felt comfortable or safe. However, God was still God. He, not Nebuchadnezzar, was in control. What situations in your life make you feel threatened and powerless? Consider God's power, goodness, and love. How could trusting in His sovereignty enable you to live in peace, even in uncertain circumstances?

5/13/15 *Right now, I am losing control of my life and it is frightening.*

Romans 15:4

"For everything that was written in the past was written to teach us, so that thru endurance and encouragement of the Scriptures we might have hope."

The Handwriting on the Wall
Daniel 5

Memorize God's Word: Romans 15:4.

❖ Daniel 5:1-4—The Great Banquet

1. Describe the setting for the events that take place in this chapter.

   Opulent - Belshazzar, Nebucadnezzar's son.

2. What did Belshazzar command according to verse 2?

   To bring the gold & silver goblets that his father took.

3. Review Daniel 1:2. Where had the vessels been kept from the time of the Jews' exile until this point?

4. What message do you think Belshazzar meant to convey by using vessels dedicated to God Almighty in the worship of his pagan gods?

❖ Daniel 5:5-12—The Writing on the Wall

5. What supernatural event interrupted the drinking party?

    _____

    _____

6. How did Belshazzar react to this interruption?

    _____

    _____

7. How did the king attempt to learn what the handwriting means?

    _____

    _____

8. What advice did the queen give Belshazzar?

    _____

    _____

9. How did the queen describe Daniel? What opinion did she seem
    to have of him?

    _____

    _____

    _____

❖ Daniel 5:13-23—A Reminder and a Reprimand

10. How did Belshazzar address Daniel in verse 13? Based on this,
    what do you think his opinion of Daniel was?

    _____

    _____

11. How did Daniel respond to the king's offer of rewards? Why do
    you think he responded this way?

    _____

    _____

12. What details from Nebuchadnezzar's life did Daniel remind Belshazzar about? (See verses 18, 19, 20, and 21.)

_____

_____

_____

13. Of what did Daniel accuse Belshazzar?

_____

_____

14. Why did Belshazzar have no excuse? (See verses 22-23.)

_____

_____

_____

❖ Daniel 5:24-28—The Interpretation of the Writing

15. What did Daniel say the words written on the wall meant?

Meneo - God has numbered the days of your reign. Tekel - you have been weighed on the scales & found wanting. Peres - your kingdom is divided & given to the Medes & Persians.

16. If Belshazzar had paid better attention to history, why would this sobering prophesy not have surprised him? (Review 2:36-39.)

Belshazzar paid no attention to what happened to his father, Nebuchadnezzar & the opulence.

17. Do you think trusting God always ensures us against physical harm or death? Why, or why not? (Also refer to John 15:18-21 and 1 Peter 2:19-25 as well as other Scriptures you may recall.)

We are to suffer for Him. Suck it up.

_____

_____

_____

❖ Daniel 5:29-31—God's Judgment Is Fulfilled

18. How did Belshazzar reward Daniel? Why did this *"gift"* end up being meaningless?

   _____

   _____

19. What judgment came to Belshazzar *"that very night"*?

   _____

   _____

20. If you have time, read Isaiah 47. Isaiah prophesied about the destruction of Babylon. Why was God upset with Babylon? How do you see this prophesy fulfilled in Daniel 1–5?

   _____

   _____

   _____

Apply what you have learned. We learned in an earlier lesson that the Babylonian name Nebuchadnezzar gave Daniel, *Belteshazzar*, means *Bel* [a pagan god] *protect him*. In this lesson, we saw King Belshazzar reminding Daniel that he was *"one of the exiles of Judah"* (5:13). If Daniel had accepted the identity these ungodly rulers tried to give him, his confidence in God might have weakened. But he didn't. Daniel always remembered who he was and who he belonged to. In the same way, the world may try to steal your true identity. Don't let that happen! You are a child of God, chosen, loved, forgiven, blessed. Is that how you see yourself? Choose to see yourself the way God sees you.

The Handwriting on the Wall
Daniel 5

In chapter 5, we see one of Nebuchadnezzar's successors, Belshazzar, learn the painful truth of Hebrews 10:31: " *It is a fearful thing to fall into the hands of the living God.*" God's full weight of judgment fell on him in a single night.

Change in Babylon's Rulers

King Nebuchadnezzar died in 562 BC. After much palace infighting and brief reigns by three kings, he was succeeded in 556 BC by Nabonidus (who later promoted his son, Belshazzar, to co-regent, placing him over the Babylonian part of the empire). Neither Nabonidus nor Belshazzar were as capable as Nebuchadnezzar. Babylon steadily declined.

The Great Banquet

Alhough enemies were gathering just outside Babylon's walls, King Belshazzar threw a lavish party (5:1). Perhaps he hoped to impress his subjects with his power and glory. After tasting the wine, Belshazzar did the unthinkable: he commanded that the sacred vessels that "*Nebuchadnezzar his father*" had taken from the temple in Jerusalem be brought in so that he and his guests could drink from them! This act showed deliberate disrespect for God. Belshazzar mocked God by using the sacred vessels from the temple of God Almighty to toast Babylon's pagan idols. (5:4).

In his unbelief, Belshazzar arrogantly brought judgment down on everyone's heads. As the banquet revelry reached a climax, the mood suddenly shifted from gaiety to terror. One of the most dramatic scenes in the Bible began to unfold (5:5-6): "*Immediately the fingers of a human hand appeared and wrote on the plaster of the wall of the king's palace,... And the king saw the hand as it wrote. Then the king's color changed, and his thoughts alarmed him; his limbs gave way, and his knees knocked together.*"

The stunned king called for Babylon's wise men. He promised that whoever interpreted the writing would *"be clothed with purple and have a chain of gold around his neck and shall be the third ruler in the kingdom"* (5:7). Purple was the color of royalty, and a gold chain symbolized high honor.

The wise men tried but could not read the handwriting (5:8) which terrified the king even more. His nobles were baffled. At this point *"the queen"* entered. Her dignity and wisdom contrasted with the drunkenness and panic that otherwise characterized the scene. She urged the king to calm himself, then offered a solution (5:10-12). She advised Belhazzar to call for Daniel, *"in whom is the spirit of the holy gods."* She reminded him that in Nebuchadnezzar's days, *"light and understanding and wisdom like the wisdom of the gods were found in him, ... An excellent spirit, knowledge, and understanding to interpret dreams, explain riddles, and solve problems were found in this Daniel, whom the king named Belteshazzar."*

Daniel Interprets the Handwriting on the Wall

Even though it had been decades since the Israelites were carried off to Babylon, Belshazzar callously reminded Daniel of his lowly status, calling him *"one of the exiles of Judah, whom the king my father brought from Judah."*

Refusing the king's promise of rewards, Daniel answered him bluntly: *"Let your gifts be for yourself, and give your rewards to another."* (5:17). The king's gifts did not motivate Daniel. Besides, given that Babylon would be destroyed in less than 24 hours, such a reward was meaningless. Still, Daniel agreed to interpret the handwriting for Belshazzar. But before he gave the interpretation, Daniel reminded the king of how God had dealt with Nebuchadnezzar for his arrogance. He charged Belshazzar with not humbling his heart, *"though you knew all this."*

Think about the value of a teachable spirit. Belshazzar knew that God rules over mankind. He knew that God had judged King Nebuchadnezzar for his arrogance. But in spite of knowing these things, he did not change. Wise people learn from history. They learn from their own mistakes and from the mistakes of others. Most of all, they fear the Lord, who is the *"beginning of wisdom"* (Proverbs 9:10). Belshazzar was not teachable. Because of this, he suffered hard consequences.

After rebuking Belshazzar, Daniel explained that the inscription on the wall announced coming judgment (5:25-28). The four words on the wall were not a secret language. They were common Aramaic words used during everyday life in Babylon. Because all the words could describe units of money that is probably how the crowd at the banquet understood them. It would be as if handwriting appeared on a wall for us and said, "$20, $20, $10, $5." This seemed ridiculous. Understandably, the interpretation eluded Belshazzar and his wise men.

Daniel explained each word. He interpreted *mene* as *numbered*, which meant that the days of Belshazzar's kingdom were numbered. God was ready to bring it to an end. He interpreted *tekel* as weighed, stating that Belshazzar had been weighed on God's scales and found lacking. The word *parsin* meant *divided or broken*. The kingdom was to be broken or divided. It would be given to the Medes and Persians.

Daniel Rewarded and the Kingdom Overthrown

Even though the interpretation Daniel supplied was negative, the terrified king kept his word. He made Daniel the third highest ruler in his kingdom (5:29-30). Perhaps Belshazzar hoped that rewarding Daniel would keep the disaster from coming. But God will not be bribed. That same night Belshazzar was killed and Darius the Mede took his place.

Think about God's control over history. Babylon did not end by chance; it ended because God had numbered its days. Our eternal God determines when one nation comes to power and another falls. Some of God's people live in nations that enjoy freedom, wealth, and security. Others live in nations wracked by poverty, oppression, and corruption. Believers who enjoy peace and security should beware of the sins of pride and presumption. God is the source of our security and well-being, not human government. In the same way, believers who do not experience these blessings do not need to feel cheated or tempted to despair. God is in control. Ultimately He *"executes justice for the oppressed* [and] *gives food to the hungry. The Lord sets the prisoners free"* (Psalm 146:7-8).

Personalize this lesson.

✓ Throughout his entire life, Daniel lived with integrity. In every situation, he faithfully obeyed God. In this lesson we saw that Belshazzar's promise of rewards did nothing to persuade Daniel. Daniel interpreted the handwriting on the wall because it was the right thing to do. He had no interest in worldly rewards. Reflect on your motivations. Ask God to reveal any motives of your heart that need His transformation. Then pray for His help. You can use Colossians 3:23-24 as a guide: "*Whatever you do, work heartily, as for the Lord and not for men, knowing that from the Lord you will receive the inheritance as your reward. You are serving the Lord Christ.*"

Daniel in the Lions' Den
Daniel 6

Memorize God's Word: Acts 5:29.

❖ Daniel 6:1-9—The Plot against Daniel

NOTE: A *satrap* was a provincial ruler.

1. Why was Daniel distinguished above the other officials?

   Daniels Trustworthy character & obedience to God. faithful

2. How did Daniel's elevated position affect the other officials'?

   Jealousy

3. What did the officials and satraps scheme against Daniel? Why did their scheme fail?

   For king Darius to issue an edict, inreversible, to pray only to the king.

4. If your conduct were to be examined as closely as Daniel's was, are there any changes you would want to make? Explain.

   More consistancy

5. Summarize the law King Darius signed.

   No one is to pray to anyone, god or man. during the next 30 days or they will be thrown into the lions' den. and 5.27.15

❖ Daniel 6:10-15—Daniel Accused

6. If your government announced a new law like the one you read about in 6:8, what would you feel? What would you do?

I pray that I would disobey.

7. What did Daniel do? What does this say about his character?

Obedient, ethical, trustworthy

8. Read 2 Chronicles 6:36-39, part of Solomon's prayer at the dedication of the temple in Jerusalem. Why was it Daniel's habit to pray in front of his window?

It was given by God to pray to the land given to them.

9. What charges did the officials bring against Daniel?

That he disobeyed the law and was praying to his God.

10. How did the king respond to these charges? Why couldn't he simply dismiss them?

He was upset, he tried to rescue Daniel all day but had to have him thrown into the lions den.

❖ Daniel 6:16-18—Daniel's Night with the Lions

11. When the king realized he was powerless to rescue Daniel from the consequences of his own law, what did he do? Do you see any hope in the situation? If so, what?

_____

_____

_____

_____

12. What was done to make sure that Daniel could not escape from the lions' den?

_____

_____

13. Compare the situation described in verse 17 with Matthew 27:57-66. How did the measures taken by officials in these two passages set the stage for God to be glorified?

_____

_____

_____

 ❖ **Daniel 6:19-24—God Rescues Daniel** 8/19/15

14. It is hard to imagine anyone surviving a night with hungry lions. Yet, the king seemed to hope for this. In these verses, how did the king express hope? On what do you think he based his hope?

_____

_____

_____

15. What did Daniel tell Darius God had done to protect him?

_____

_____

16. You may recall from lesson 2 that Daniel's name means *God is my judge.* How does he live true to the meaning of his name?

_____

_____

_____

17. How do the details described in verse 24 help to prove that Daniel's rescue was a miracle?

_____

_____

❖ **Daniel 6:25-28—Daniel Exalts God** 4\19\15

18. How did Darius describe Daniel's God?

_____

_____

19. Review 2:46-47, 3:28-29, 4:2-3, and 4:34-35. What similarities
do you find between this passage and the one in 6:26-27?

_____

_____

20. Based on your study of Daniel in general and these passages in
particular, what would you say is the theme of this book? What
point is being made about God?

_____

_____

_____

God in control

Apply what you have learned. It was Daniel's
habit to pray three times a day. How often and
regularly do you talk to God? It's fine to pray
spontaneously, whenever you need His help. But it is also
important to pray at regular times, like Daniel did. Such a
practice keeps us more firmly connected to God. It matures
and strengthens us in our faith. Why not commit to a pray at
three regular times each day during the remainder of this
study? Look at your schedule. Pick three times you can
intentionally stop to pray each day. Then do as Daniel did:
pray and thank God during those times.

Start 26?

Daniel in the Lions' Den
Daniel 6

This week's study reminds us of God's awesome power and sovereignty. Like the chapters before it, Daniel 6 recounts a vivid story of faith and courage in a pagan culture. The aged Daniel, probably in his 80s, stood for what he believed, despite the consequences. And God miraculously delivered him!

The Plot against Daniel

Darius began his rule by appointing 120 satraps (governors) over Babylon. Over the satraps he appointed three administrators (6:1-2). These administrators, one of whom was Daniel, reported directly to the king. Daniel's talent, experience, and integrity quickly distinguished him. Because of the *"excellent spirit"* he showed, Darius planned to *"set him over the whole kingdom"* (6:3).

Daniel's promotion provoked the other officials. They looked for a way to remove him. As in chapter 3, they probably were jealous. Possibly they also were prejudiced against Jewish outsiders. In contrast to other kingdom officials, Daniel was honest and trustworthy. Daniel's integrity probably angered his peers and subordinates who may have accepted bribes and used deception to get things done. Yet despite their effort, they could found no fault with Daniel.

Finally, the scheming officials thought of a deceitful plot to eliminate Daniel (6:7-8). They knew that Daniel regularly prayed to God. He had been doing so for as long as anyone could remember. So they approached the king with flattery. They suggested a 30-day period in which all prayer would be dedicated to him alone. Secretly, of course, their purpose was to discredit Daniel.

Daniel and the Lions

Daniel refused to change his practice, even though he knew it might cost him his life. As soon as the document was signed, he went to his house where he had windows in his upper chamber open toward Jerusalem. He got down on his knees three times a day and prayed and gave thanks before his God, as he had done previously (6:10).

Think about religious rights. When laws are passed that infringe upon people's religious freedoms, they tend to be upset—and rightfully so. Often there are public outcries: petitions, sit-ins, boycotts, marches, and angry comments spread over social media. But Daniel's response is different from these typical responses in our contemporary society. There is no indication that Daniel protested or made any effort to change the law. Rather, he quietly submitted himself to God, praying as he had always prayed, allowing God to be his judge and defender. Why do you suppose Daniel responded this way? What does his example suggest to you about how to respond when your religious freedoms are threatened?

Although Daniel's service to the Persian government was faultless, his enemies used his faith to persecute him. They were delighted to see Daniel violate the king's new law by continuing his regular routine of daily prayer.

Eager to see Daniel punished, the officials hurried to Darius. They told him, *"Daniel, who is one of the exiles from Judah, pays no attention to you, O king, or the injunction you have signed, but makes his petition three times a day"* (6:13).

Darius was greatly distressed. But he was trapped. According to the law, he could not revoke the injunction he had signed. Darius regarded Daniel highly. He probably realized that his officials had maliciously tricked him.

The text says that *"the king ... set his mind to deliver Daniel. And he labored till the sun went down to rescue him"* (6:14). But the law of the Medes and Persians was irrevocable. He had no choice but to throw Daniel to the lions.

Reluctantly, Darius ordered Daniel's punishment. But first he spoke to Daniel, saying, *"May your God, whom you serve continually, deliver you!"*

(6:16). Then he put a stone over the den and sealed the entrance with his signet ring. The seal guaranteed that no one could rescue Daniel secretly.

God Rescues and Vindicates Daniel

Darius refused to eat or enjoy entertainment all evening. He did not sleep all night. At dawn's first light, he hurried to the lions' den. When he got there, he cried out in anguish, "*O Daniel, servant of the living God, has your God, whom you serve continually, been able to deliver you from the lions?*" (6:20). And learned that Daniel was alive!

Daniel answered, "*O king, live forever! My God sent His angel and shut the lions' mouths, and they have not harmed me, because I was found blameless before Him; and also before you, O king, I have done no harm*" (6:21-22).

Daniel's survival was completely miraculous. We would expect that the lions would have attacked Daniel the minute he was thrown in. Later, Darius threw Daniel's enemies into the pit as justice for their evil scheme. Before they had even fallen to the den's floor, the lions viciously attacked them (6:24). But because of God's incredible protection, hungry lions left Daniel untouched for a whole night.

Think about God's sovereignty. The theme of the book of Daniel can be summed up as, "No matter how bad things get, God is still in control." God cares for Daniel's personal well-being in the various risky situations he finds himself. God rules over kings and nations. He causes one to fall and another to rise. We will continue to see this theme play out in the remaining chapters of Daniel, as God reveals mysteries to Daniel about the distant future. Things are going to get pretty bad on the world scene, but do not fear, God is still in control!

The King Praises Daniel's God

The king was delighted to have Daniel back as his trusted servant. He also recognized the power of Daniel's God. He issued a government decree that all those in his kingdom were "*to tremble and fear before the God of Daniel*" (6:26). Because of Daniel's influence, Darius made a public declaration of the power and permanence of God's kingdom.

Personalize this lesson.

It's easy to start a race, but a lot harder to finish it. Daniel, however, provides a wonderful example of both starting and ending his spiritual life well. Throughout his entire life he remained faithful to God. As a teenager, he was completely devoted to his God. And as an elderly man, he continued in that loyal devotion, praying, serving, and honoring God without regard for what it might cost. Does your spiritual life have the same vigor now as it had when you first began your life with God? What do you need to do to ensure that you will finish well later in life?

A Vision of Beasts, a Ram, and a Goat
Daniel 7– 8

❖ Daniel 7:1-8—Daniel's Vision of the Beasts

Read chapter 7 to get a general idea of Daniel's vision. Then concentrate on verses 1-8.

1. Describe the first beast Daniel saw in his vision and what happened to it.

   Like a lion, w/ wings of an eagle - the wings were torn off - lifted & stood on 2 ft. / a heart of a man was given to it.

2. What did the second best look like, and what was it told to do?

   Like a bear, raised up an its sides w/ 3 ribs in his mouth between its teeth - Get up & eat your fill of flesh.

3. What did the third beast look like and what was it given?

   Like a leopard, on his back 4 wings like a bird's 4 heads / it was given authority to rule.

4. What was the fourth beast that Daniel saw like?

   "Terrifying & frightening & very powerful / lg. iron teeth crushed & devoured its victims & trampled underfoot what was left / 10 horns / then another horn, a little one 3 of the 1st horns were uprooted. This horn had eyes like a man & a boastful mouth

❖ Daniel 7:9-14—Daniel's Vision of Judgment

5. How would you describe what Daniel saw next in his vision (verses 9-10)?

    God the Father with believers surrounding him & worshipping. Possibly at the end of time.

6. What happened to the fourth beast as Daniel watched?

7. How did Daniel describe the person he saw next (verses 13-14)?

8. Read the following verses from the New Testament: Mark 14:60-62; Revelation 1:7, 12-18. Who is this person?

❖ Daniel 7:15-28—The Interpretation of the Vision

9. According to 7:16-18, what did Daniel's vision mean?

10. Ultimately, what would happen to the fourth beast?

11. Who will rule in the end? For how long?

❖ Daniel 8:1-14—Vision of a Ram and a Goat

12. What two animals did Daniel see and what did they do?

_____

_____

13. How did Daniel describe the little horn and what it did?

_____

_____

14. What do think the term *"the glorious land"* refers to? (See Ezekiel 20:5-6.)

_____

_____

15. What would the little horn do with truth? Why does this matter? (Consider John 8:32; 18:37.)

_____

_____

❖ Daniel 8:15-27—The Small Horn

16. According to Gabriel, who or what do each of the following from Daniel's vision represent: the ram, the goat, the horn between the goat's eyes, the four horns, the little horn (see also verses 8-9)?

_____

_____

_____

17. When would the events Daniel sees in his vision take place? (See verses 17, 19, and 26.)

_____

_____

18. How does this passage hint at the truth that even in evil times, God is still in control? (See verses 22 and 25-26.)

_____

_____

_____

_____

Apply what you have learned. Jesus called the devil *"the father of lies"* (John 8:44) for good reason. One of the enemy's prime tactics is to *"throw truth to the ground"* (Daniel 8:12). He wants to discredit God so we won't trust Him or give Him the honor He deserves. He'll do this in the last days, but he's also does it now. We need to be on guard. Ask God to reveal any places where the enemy has lied to you about God's character. Has he planted seeds of doubt about God's goodness, love, or right to rule? Has he tried to convince you that God is mad at you, that He won't take care of you, or that He is eager to punish you for making mistakes? If God reveals any of the devil's lies to you, confess them! Ask God to show you the truth, then ask Him to help you to live in that truth. Remember, Jesus said, *"You will know the truth, and the truth will set you free"* (John 8:32).

Lesson 9 Commentary

A Vision of Beasts, a Ram, and a Goat
Daniel 7–8

Daniel 7–12 shifts from describing events during Daniel's life to his visions of the future. As you study these last six chapters, remember that no one has all the answers to what these prophecies mean. It is far more important to understand that no matter how bad things around us become, we can be confident that our good God is in control of the course and outcome of world history.

Daniel's Vision of the Four Beasts

The vision occurred "*in the first year of Belshazzar king of Babylon.*" Belshazzar began reigning as co-regent with his father in 553 BC, so chronologically, the vision in chapter 7 precedes the events of chapter 5. Belshazzar proved to be an incompetent king. He was a pagan who had no respect for the true God. Daniel and the Jewish people must have felt alarmed over his rise to power. Daniel's vision, therefore, was timely and encouraging. It acknowledged the trials of God's people under evil regimes. It also declared the final victory of God and those who worship Him.

Daniel received these revelations through a dream. In his dream he saw four different beasts coming up out of the sea. The first was like a lion that had the wings of an eagle. The next beast, "*like a bear*" fits the description of the Medo-Persian Empire, which succeeded Babylon. The powerful, plodding bear pictures how Persia's armies methodically overwhelmed their foes.

The third beast appeared, "*like a leopard, with four wings of a bird on its back. And the beast had four heads, and dominion was given to it.*" Many scholars believe this beast corresponds to Alexander the Great and the Greek Empire. Alexander's armies were famous for their lightning speed, pictured by the four wings and the leopard. The four heads could portray the division of Alexander's vast empire among his four generals after his death.

The final beast was terrifying, dreadful, strong, and different from the other beasts. Scholars differ on their interpretation of what this beast represents. It seems to parallel the legs and feet of the statue in Daniel 2.

The vision of the statue and the vision of the beasts have been similar so far, but now a new twist is added—the little horn that resembles a person.

The Ancient of Days and the Son of Man

While Daniel contemplated his vision, the scene changed. It was breathtaking. He saw thrones and on one of them, "*The Ancient of Days took His seat; His clothing was white as snow, and the hair of His head like pure wool.*" It was a courtroom scene where books were opened and people were judged. The Judge was called the "*Ancient of Days.*" He sat on a throne that was brilliant with streams of fire. Daniel's vision portrays God as the final Judge of humanity. Thousands serve Him; He is magnificent, eternal, and all-powerful.

However, even in the presence of the Ancient of Days, the little horn continued its boasting. But not for long. As Daniel watched, "*the beast was killed, and its body destroyed and given over to be burned with fire.*"

Think about our hope. Our hope does not rest in governments, national leaders, or world powers. Human leadership is flawed at best—and godless, corrupt, and tyrannical at worst. But human governments do not have the final say—God does! He is the one who will ultimately put all evil to rest. He will rule in justice. He will rescue and vindicate all who have suffered for His sake. Instead of fretting over evil, David invites us to "*trust in the LORD and do good*" (Psalm 37:3).

Now comes one of the Bible's most astonishing scenes (7:13-14): Daniel saw "*one like a Son of Man*" coming with the clouds of heaven and being presented to the Ancient of Days. This Son of Man was given an everlasting kingdom that would never be destroyed.

The Interpretation of the Vision

Perplexed, Daniel asked an angel to explain. The angel told him that the beasts represented four kings of the earth—but eventually, God's people would possess His final kingdom forever. The angel said that the fourth beast was a fourth kingdom, different from all the others (7:23): *"He shall speak words against the Most High, and shall wear out the saints of the Most High, and shall think to change the times and the law; and they shall be given into his hand."*

Think about the enemy's strategies. Temptation to sin isn't the only way he tries to trap us. He also tries to discourage us. He tries to *"wear out the saints of the Most High"* (7:25) so we will give up in defeat. That's probably why God so often calls us to perseverance and patient endurance (see Hebrews 10:36 and Revelation 13:10, 14:12). On our own, we don't have the strength. But God will give us the power we need so the enemy can't wear us out.

A Second Vision

Daniel received a second, similar vision approximately two years after the first one. Both visions involved animals that represented subsequent kingdoms. But God gave more specific interpretation to the second vision.

In the vision, Daniel saw himself in Susa, about 350 miles east of Babylon. He saw a two-horned ram standing on the bank of the Ulai canal. A goat with an unusual horn entered the picture. Later in the chapter, Gabriel told Daniel that the two-horned ram represented the kings of Media and Persia; the goat represented the king of Greece. He said that the four horns that replaced the single broken horn represented four kingdoms that would rise out of Greece (8:20-22). Gabriel's explanation foretold what would happen over the next 250 years when the swift Greek conquests under Alexander the Great dealt the Persian Empire its death blow in 331 BC.

The next part of Daniel's vision involved a little horn that grew out of one of the goat's four horns. (8:9-10). As Daniel watched, he saw the regular burnt offering taken away from the Prince of the host and his sanctuary overthrown. The small horn threw truth to the ground—and in all this, it prospered. This prophecy mentioned a specific person who appeared to be descended from one of the four horns, or generals, who would divide Alexander's empire. He extended his power to *"the glorious land,"* which probably refers to Israel. The most important thing to remember is that evil's triumph is short-lived. God will always win in the end.

Personalize this lesson.

In the first half of Daniel, we found him encountering trials that had life-and-death implications. Yet in none of these did he seem flustered, anxious, or afraid. He seemed to take everything in stride. But now, in chapters 7 and 8, we see him overcome with emotion. He was anxious and alarmed (7:15, 28); terrified (7:19); frightened (8:17); appalled; and even physically sick with emotion (8:27). Why do you suppose Daniel was so emotional about things affecting God's kingdom? What things most deeply affect your heart? What does this show about your trust in God? Ask God for any heart changes you may need.

Daniel's Prayer
Daniel 9

Memorize God's Word: 2 Chronicles 7:14.

❖ Daniel 9:1-3—Daniel's Discovery

1. What important discovery did Daniel make during the first year of Darius' reign (between 539 and 538 BC)?

   _____

   _____

   _____

2. How did Daniel respond to his discovery? Why do you think he responded this way?

   _____

   _____

   _____

   _____

3. Are there times when you read something in Scripture that you realize applies specifically to you? How does Daniel's example inspire you to respond in times like that?

   _____

   _____

   _____

   _____

Ppm 117
Praise

❖ Daniel 9:4-15—Daniel Offers Praise and Confession to God

4. Read Daniel's prayer carefully. Notice all the expressions of praise and worship. What attributes and characteristics of God does He mention?

   _____

   _____

   _____

   _____

5. What would you like to learn from Daniel about including praise and worship in your prayers to God?

   The Lords prayer _____

   _____

   _____

   _____

6. From Jeremiah 25:1-11, what message had God sent to Israel through His prophets and how had Israel responded?

   _____

   _____

   _____

7. What was God's resulting judgment on Israel? Why was it just?

   _____

   _____

   _____

   _____

8. In Daniel 9:11, how did Daniel summarize Israel's sin?

   _____

   _____

   _____

9. Notice that Daniel used the plural, personal pronouns *we* and *us* in making his confession. Why do you suppose Daniel said *we* and *us* instead of *they* and *them*? How did his inclusion of himself inspire as you pray concerning sins of the communities you are part of?

    _____

    _____

❖ Daniel 9:16-19—Daniel's Petition

10. What, specifically, did Daniel ask God to do for Israel?

    _____

    _____

11. Daniel showed great concern for God's glory. List all the examples of this that you can find in these verses.

    _____

    _____

    _____

12. What conclusions about prayer could you draw from 9:20-23? (See also Psalm 66:16-20; James 5:16-18.)

    _____

    _____

    _____

❖ Daniel 9:20-23—Gabriel Brings an Answer

13. What was Daniel doing when Gabriel came to him?

    _____

    _____

14. Why did Gabriel say he had come to Daniel?

    _____

    _____

15. What did Gabriel say to encourage Daniel?

_____

_____

❖ Daniel 9:24-27—The 70 Weeks

16. According to 9:24, what six accomplishments would be completed by the end of the 70 *"weeks"*?

_____

_____

_____

_____

17. What would happen after the 62 weeks?

_____

_____

18. What does Daniel 9:26 say would continue to the end?

_____

_____

Apply what you have learned. Daniel prayed for his people and his nation. He began his prayer with praise. He continued with confession, and finished with a plea for mercy and for God's name to be honored. How might you use Daniel's prayer as a model to pray for your nation or for God's people this week?

Daniel's Prayer
Daniel 9

In this chapter, we get a glimpse into Daniel's prayer life. We see his close relationship with God. We see Daniel studying Scripture then turning to God in fasting and prayer. He asked God to forgive the sins of his people. God answered quickly. He sent the angel Gabriel to give Daniel encouragement and promises for the future. These prophecies remind us that no matter what happens, God will bring His *"everlasting righteousness."*

Daniel's Discovery

The events of chapter 9 took place in the first year of Darius's reign. Historians believe this was probably between 539 and 538 BC. It was a little more than a decade after the vision Daniel recorded in chapter 8. Chronologically, chapter 9 follows 5:31. Daniel was an old man, perhaps 80 years of age.

We find Daniel engrossed in the Scriptures. He was reading the book of Jeremiah. As he was reading, he *"perceived in the books the number of years that, according to the word of the Lord to Jeremiah the prophet, must pass before the end of the desolations of Jerusalem, namely, seventy years"* (verse 2). As Daniel studied, he came to 29:10, which promised that God would return the displaced Israelites to their land: *"When seventy years are completed for Babylon, I will visit you, and I will fulfill to you My promise and bring you back to this place."* Babylon had recently been conquered. Nearly seven decades had passed since Daniel's captivity began in 605 BC. Daniel realized that the Jews' return to Jerusalem was approaching.

With God's Word encouraging his faith, Daniel decided to pray. God had made promises to Israel, assuring them that they would not be in exile forever. However, Daniel also realized that Israel needed to repent. Many of the Israelites had not yet acknowledged the sins that sent them into captivity.

So Daniel humbled himself before God. He fasted, put on sackcloth, and poured ashes on his head. In these ways he symbolized his sorrow over sin. He was genuinely grieved over the state of his people and his land.

Think about the relationship between Scripture and prayer. Daniel's Bible reading prompted his prayer. The promises of Scripture inspired Daniel's praise, confession, and petition. Daniel's prayer is rich and theologically solid because he was well acquainted with God's Word. What part does Scripture have in your prayer life?

Daniel's Prayer

Daniel was a man of prayer (see 2:18, 6:10-13). He confessed that Israel had sinned. They had rejected God's commands, even though He had sent many prophets to warn them. Daniel did not set himself above his fellow Israelites. Daniel lived righteously before God. But he knew that he had failed God, too. So instead of blaming the idol-worshipers and rebels, he confessed his sin along with theirs.

Daniel praised God's righteousness, mercy, and forgiveness. God's holiness sharply contrasted with Israel's rebellion and shame. Daniel understood that Israel deserved God's judgment. Daniel began to plead for mercy (9:16-19). God had promised to deliver His people. He said He would return them to their homeland. God said He would be merciful. So Daniel specifically asked God to restore His people, His city, and His temple.

Think about Daniel's motivation in prayer. He was God-focused. It is true that Israel was oppressed. The Israelites had experienced hardship at the hands of pagan, oppressive rulers. But Daniel did not ask God for Israel's comfort. He asked God to glorify Himself. He was concerned for God's reputation. So Daniel pleaded for the city and the people that *"are called by Your name."* It is all right to ask God for comfort, safety, and smooth paths. But how different might our prayers be if our primary focus were God, His reputation, and His glory?

God's Sends Gabriel

Daniel had barely finished saying the words, *"Delay not"* when the angel Gabriel appeared to him. God heard Daniel's prayer and answered him almost immediately. Gabriel appeared *"at the time of the evening sacrifice"* (3 p.m.). It is interesting that Daniel included this detail. Because sacrifices could be offered only at the temple in Jerusalem, there could have been no evening sacrifice offered for nearly 70 years. But we know that Daniel prayed at set times every day (6:10). It would not surprise us, then, that he set those times based on the sacrificial schedule. This would be one way to remember God's holy requirements and provision for sin.

Gabriel came *"in swift flight"* at this specific time. He gave Daniel insight and understanding and told Daniel that he was greatly loved. Daniel must have been deeply encouraged to hear those reassuring words. How good it would have been for him to know that God had heard and received his prayer.

The 70 Weeks

First, Gabriel affirmed and reassured Daniel. Then he offered the insight he had promised. His explanation was puzzling, however. Gabriel told Daniel about 70 weeks that would be important to Israel's future. During this time, six things would happen: transgressions would be finished, an end would be put to sin, iniquity would be atoned for, everlasting righteousness would be brought in, vision and prophet would be sealed, and a most holy place would be anointed.

"Weeks" does not seem to mean time periods of seven 24-hour days, as we commonly use the word. Many scholars understand *weeks* to mean *years*. But scholars disagree over what the 70 weeks refer to specifically. Whatever the details may look like, the promises God gave in 9:24 were encouraging. Knowing that God would *"put an end to sin"* and *"bring in everlasting righteousness"* must have given Daniel hope. These promises described future peace for the nation and a final victory for God.

Verse 25 explains when the 70 weeks would begin: *"From the going out of the word to restore and build Jerusalem to the coming of an anointed one, a prince, there shall be seven weeks."* Disagreements over the interpretation 9:24-27 have led to confusion and conflict among Christians. But we do not need to know the precise interpretation and timing of these events. It is more important for us to understand the theme Daniel continually puts before us: God's people can expect opposition, but God will triumph in the end!

Personalize this lesson.

☑ In his prayer, Daniel points out that God had sent prophets to warn the Israelites to turn from their sin and obey Him. But they did not listen. God sometimes gives us warnings, too. He may warn us through His Word, the Holy Spirit, or through pastors, teachers, family members, and friends who care for us spiritually. Pause and ask God to bring to mind any warnings He has given you. Have you followed up on what He has said to you? If not, confess it to Him. Ask Him for greater trust, humility, diligence—and His power to obey. Your humble obedience will bring pleasure to God.

Spiritual Warfare
Daniel 10:1–11:35

❖ Daniel 10:1-3—Daniel Mourns

1. Compare 10:1 with Ezra 1:1-4. What context do the verses from Ezra provide?

    _____

    _____

2. Why do you think Daniel remained in Persia, even after the Jews were permitted to return to Jerusalem?

    _____

    _____

3. What had Daniel been doing for three weeks? Why do you suppose he had been doing this?

    _____

    _____

❖ Daniel 10:4-9—Daniel Sees a Vision

4. Describe the man Daniel saw on the banks of the Tigris River.

    _____

    _____

5. Who do you think this man was? Explain your answer.

    _____

    _____

6. What effect did this vision have on Daniel?

_____

_____

7. How did the vision affect the men who were with Daniel?

_____

_____

❖ Daniel 10:10-13—Spiritual Conflict

8. What did the messenger do and say to reassure Daniel?

_____

_____

_____

9. When was Daniel's prayer first heard, according to the messenger?

_____

10. How long had it taken the messenger to bring the answer?

_____

_____

11. What accounted for the delay?

_____

_____

12. What information do the following passages give concerning spiritual conflict?

   a. Luke 22:31 _____

   _____

   b. 2 Corinthians 2:11 _____

   _____

   c. Ephesians 6:10-18 _____

   _____

d. 1 Peter 5:8-9 _____

_____

13. How does knowing about the reality of spiritual conflict affect your thoughts about prayer?

_____

_____

14. How does knowing about the reality of spiritual conflict affect your perspective about delays, obstacles, trials, or temptations?

_____

_____

❖ Daniel 10:14–11:4—Persia and Greece

15. How did Daniel respond to what the messenger told him?

_____

_____

16. How did the messenger tangibly help Daniel?

_____

17. What did the messenger explain to Daniel?

_____

_____

❖ Daniel 11:5-35—Antiochus Epiphanes' Campaigns

Note: This section contains numerous prophecies about the nations surrounding Israel. In the Commentary we will learn how these prophecies have been fulfilled. It is okay if you do not understand all the details as you study this section. Simply focus on what stands out to you as interesting.

18. Read verses 5-9. What stands out to you from this passage?

_____

_____

_____

19. Read verses 10-19. What stands out to you from this passage?

_____

_____

_____

20. Read verses 20-28. What stands out to you from this passage?

_____

_____

_____

21. Read verses 29-35. What stands out to you from this passage?

_____

_____

_____

Apply what you have learned. When most of us read prophecy, we want to know, "When will this happen? Will it affect me?" But whether a prophecy affects us directly or not, God has important principles we can learn from it. For example, although the prophecies in Daniel 11 were fulfilled prior to 164 BC, we can still learn from them. We learn in 11:32 that in times of trial and oppression, "*the people who know their God shall stand firm and take action.*" And in 11:33 we see that "*the wise among the people shall make many understand.*" The trials we face may not be as severe as the ones Daniel wrote about. But we all face trials. Think of a trial you are currently experiencing. Are you standing firm? Is there action God is calling you to take?

Lesson 11 Commentary

Spiritual Warfare
Daniel 10:1–11:35

We come now to Daniel's fourth and final vision. A heavenly being enabled Daniel to see behind the scenes. Daniel witnessed a spiritual conflict taking place. Then, in chapter 11, the messenger shared specific prophecies concerning Israel and the nations surrounding her. Most scholars believe these prophecies have already been fulfilled. How good it is to know that every word of God is true, and every promise He makes will be fulfilled!

A Messenger Appears to Daniel

The events of Daniel 10 took place in the third year of Cyrus, King of Persia. Daniel was still in Persia, which seems a bit surprising. Two years earlier Cyrus had decreed that the Jews could return to Israel. So why did he remain in Persia? We can only speculate, since the text does not tell us. Perhaps it is simply that he was an old man now, and the trip would have been too difficult. Regardless, God clearly had work left for Daniel to do in Persia.

Daniel had been fasting and mourning for three weeks. As Daniel stood on the bank of the Tigris River, he saw an awesome being. The being looked like a man, but his body was like beryl (a transparent green or yellow gemstone). His face was "*like the appearance of lightning, his eyes like flaming torches, his arms and legs like the gleam of burnished bronze, and the sound of his words like the sound of a multitude*" (10:4-6).

Who was this remarkable being? Again, the text does not say. Scholars have debated whether he was a powerful angel, or whether he might even have been a theophany (a visible appearance of God in human form). Either way, Daniel was stunned. He lost all his strength and fell to the ground, face first, in deep sleep.

The mysterious messenger strengthened and calmed Daniel. His personal touch comforted Daniel so he could get up onto his hands and knees—but he was still shaking. So the messenger reassured him. He told Daniel that he was *"greatly loved."* He urged Daniel to stand to his feet. Daniel, still trembling, obeyed. The messenger reassured Daniel even further: *"Fear not, Daniel, for from the first day that you set your heart to understand and humbled yourself before your God, your words have been heard, and I have come because of your words"* (10:12).

Then the heavenly being explained why he had failed to come sooner: *"The prince of the kingdom of Persia withstood me twenty-one days"* (verse 13).

Think about the timing of answered prayer. In chapter 9, Daniel had not even finished praying when Gabriel, the angel, appeared (9:20-23). In chapter 10 he had been praying for three weeks before God's answer came. In both cases, however, God heard Daniel's prayer as soon as he prayed it. But the answers to his prayers came at different times. God hears our prayers, we know that. But some answers will take longer than others. The important thing is to keep waiting for Him, just like Daniel did.

Who was this *"prince of the kingdom of Persia"* who delayed the answer to Daniel's prayer? Again, the text gives no explanation. But no human prince could possibly restrain an angel, so the *"prince of the kingdom of Persia"* seems to have been an evil angel. The Bible teaches that God created an invisible angelic world but that some of the angels rebelled against Him, much as Adam and Eve did. The rebellious angels became evil. The leader of the evil angels is Satan himself. The evil *"prince of the kingdom of Persia"* delayed God's messenger from coming to Daniel, but only for three weeks. Ultimately, he could not prevent God's purposes from being carried out.

Think about large-scale spiritual warfare strategy. The enemy is not only concerned with destroying individuals—he seeks to deceive entire nations (see Revelation 20:3). Sometimes we complain about government authorities, thinking they are our enemies. But that is no solution. Rather than criticizing the leaders we disagree with, it would be much better to talk to God about them. We never see Daniel slandering or defaming the ungodly leaders he lived under. Instead, he prayed for them.

Persia and Greece

Finally, Daniel was composed enough to listen. The messenger asked him, *"Do you know why I have come to you?"* (10:20). Daniel did not give a reply, and the messenger continued without waiting for one. We can only guess how Daniel might have answered the messenger's question. One possibility is that the messenger came simply because Daniel prayed. This idea is supported in 10:12. The messenger explained that he would soon leave to fight against the prince of Persia. Then he would fight against the prince of Greece, who was apparently another evil angel. Before he left, however, the angel told Daniel what was written *"in the book of truth,"* which was possibly a symbolic reference to a divine record in heaven.

Kings of the South and the North

Antiochus IV Epiphanes was ruthless and manipulative. This was true of many kings of the North and the South who had ruled over Israel during previous decades. But this tyrant would be even more oppressive. He planned to unite his unstable empire by imposing Greek religion and culture on all his subjects. He might allow the Jews some form of worship of their own God, but they also would have to worship his god, Zeus. Other kings had given them freedom of worship. He would not. Antiochus and the Jews were headed toward conflict. But Antiochus did not know what he is getting himself into. God would not permit the extermination of either the Jewish faith or the Jewish people. As we saw in chapter 10, God's angels were working behind the scenes. The Lord raised up resistance to this evil ruler (11:32-33).

Personalize this lesson.

☑ Daniel's encounter with the heavenly messenger—who may have been the Lord Himself—completely overwhelmed him. All his strength left him. He fell face to the ground in deep sleep. Even when the messenger touched him and reassured him, he continued to tremble. God invites us into intimate, personal friendship with Him. However, God is also Holy (see Isaiah 57:15). In which way do you most often relate to God? With holy and reverent fear? Or with comfortable intimacy? This week, try relating to Him in the way that is less familiar to you.

Lesson 12

Deliverance for God's People
Daniel 11:36–12:13

Memorize God's Word: Daniel: 12:2-3.

❖ Daniel 11:36-39—The King Who Will Do as He Wills

1. From verses 36-38, list every bad characteristic you can find about this evil king.

   Self centered, arrogant
   _____
   _____

2. From your list in question 1, which trait about the evil king troubles you most? Why?

   _____
   _____

3. Read Psalm 20:7 and Isaiah 31:1. What is wrong with honoring *"the god of fortresses"*?

   _____
   _____

❖ Daniel 11:40-45—The Fall of the Evil King

4. From verse 40, when will the military campaigns described in these verses take place?

   _____
   _____

5. Where will the evil king come into, according to verse 41?

_____

_____

_____

6. According to verses 44-45, the king initiates a final campaign. Why? How does it turn out?

_____

_____

_____

❖ Daniel 12:1—A Time of Trouble

7. Who arises at this time of great trouble, according to 12:1? How is he described?

_____

_____

_____

8. Who will be delivered during this terrible time?

_____

_____

9. Read Revelation 20:12, 15 and 21:27. What is the significance of "*the book*" mentioned in verse 1?

_____

_____

_____

10. Is your name written in that book? How do you know?

_____

_____

_____

_____

❖ Daniel 12:2-4—The Resurrection of the Dead

11. What do you think it means that *"those who sleep in the dust of the earth shall awake"*?

    _____

    _____

12. What are the two different destinies described for those who will *"awake"*?

    _____

    _____

    _____

13. Read John 5:24-29 and John 11:25-26. What determines the destiny of those who are resurrected?

    _____

    _____

    _____

❖ Daniel 12:5-13—Unanswered Questions

14. From verse 8, what did Daniel ask?

    _____

    _____

15. What answer was Daniel given?

    _____

    _____

16. Do you think the answer satisfied him? Why or why not?

    _____

    _____

    _____

    _____

17. Why do you think so many people are eager to know what the future holds?

_____

_____

_____

_____

18. Why do you think God doesn't tell us all the details about the future ahead of time?

_____

_____

_____

_____

Apply what you have learned. Are you in a *"time of trouble"*? When times of trouble come, it helps to remember that they have purpose. Wise people will allow God to use trials to purify and refine them. Wicked people, on the other hand, just continue to act wickedly. They gain nothing from their painful experiences (12:10). God's Word promises that *"suffering produces endurance, and endurance produces character, and character produces hope"* (Romans 5:4). What trouble are you currently facing? Talk to God about it. Ask Him for whatever you need from Him in order to stand firm and come through strong.

Deliverance for God's People
Daniel 11:36–12:13

Our final lesson contains more unexplained prophecy. Even when Daniel asked for answers, he received only vague replies. However, the text makes some things very clear: evil will not always triumph. God will come. He will reign victoriously. And His faithful people will come safely through their trials into life everlasting.

We do not know the identity of the evil king described in Daniel 11:36-45. Many scholars believe that it could not be Antiochus IV Epiphanes, for reasons we will discuss. Otherwise, we can only guess. So we need to be humble and open as we study. However, we can be sure about this: for people who truly love God, the world can be a hostile place. But God has given us everything we need to overcome.

The King Who Will Do as He Wills

If we looked at the text only, we might assume Daniel was speaking of the same king (whom history identifies as Antiochus IV Epiphanes) that he described starting in 11:21. However, as we continue reading and comparing with what we know from history, it seems this might actually be a different king. Much within 11:36-45 does not correspond historically with what we know of Antiochus. Reformer John Calvin believed this evil king was a personification of the Roman Empire. Other scholars believed he was Herod. Still others believed he was a leader of one of the great world religions. Other theories have circulated as well.

Many contemporary interpreters believe this is a final antichrist who will come at the close of history. They connect descriptions in Daniel 7, 8, 11, and 12, with John's descriptions of the beast in Revelation (e.g. Revelation 13:14). They also connect this person with Paul's descriptions of *"the man of lawlessness"* (2 Thessalonians 2:3-4, 8).

This king could in fact be Christ's chief opponent at the end of history. Or he could represent one of the Lord's many enemies throughout history. We cannot be positive about the identity (or identities) of this mysterious person. However, we can learn the lessons from these verses that apply to every generation. For example, this king *"shall exalt himself and magnify himself above every god.... he shall magnify himself above all."* But God hates arrogance and pride (Proverbs 8:13). This king *"shall speak astonishing things against the God of gods."* But God punishes blasphemy and honors those who reverence and fear the Lord. Also, this king *"shall honor the god of fortresses."* But God judges those who *"rely on horses, who trust in chariots ... but do not look to the Holy One of Israel, or consult the Lord!"* (Isaiah 31:1).

Ultimately, this exceptionally evil king proved weaker than he appeared. Evil may seem to have the upper hand for a time, but God always triumphs in the end. God's victory is everlasting.

Think about one of the main themes of Daniel: God is in control. No matter how bad things seem, God is still in charge. He will win in the end. When we believe that nothing happens apart from God, and that He works all things together for good, we can live with hope. We do not have to live in fear and defeat.

Deliverance for God's People

Chapter 11 closes with God defeating his chief enemy. In chapter 12 Michael, one of God's mightiest angels, reappeared. While the king who does as he pleases was wreaking havoc on Israel and the world, Michael, the great archangel, was behind the scenes, guarding God's people. We met Michael earlier in Daniel 10:13, 21. He was described there as one of the chief princes and *"your prince."* This description suggests that God assigned Michael to protect His people.

Think about the ministry of angels. For such a relatively short book in Scripture, Daniel refers surprisingly often to angels. In Scripture, references to the archangels Michael and Gabriel are extremely rare. But Daniel contains multiple references to both as they protect, guide, encourage, and instruct Daniel and his people. Most of us will never see angels with our physical eyes. However, Daniel is a good reminder that God has commanded these "*ministering spirits*" to serve His people (Hebrews 1:14).

In the midst of this time of great trouble, God's people will overcome. God will deliver those whose names are "*written in the book.*" This "*book*" is the Lamb's book of life (see Revelation 13:8; 20:12, 15; 21:27). This deliverance may or may not be physical. God does not promise physical deliverance from every trial. There have been martyrs in nearly every generation throughout history. But we can be sure that this deliverance is spiritual. No one whose name is written in the book of life will be eternally lost. Because they put their trust in Jesus, they belong to Him forever. No one can "*snatch them out of the Father's hand*" (John 10:29).

Verse 2 is one of the most important verses about the resurrection of the dead in the entire Old Testament. It describes believers' resurrection to eternal life. It also says that nonbelievers will experience eternal destruction. Believers will receive wonderful new bodies, free from disease and imperfections, to complete their salvation (1 Corinthians 15:42-44; Revelation 21:4). Nonbelievers also will rise from the dead (Revelation 20:11-15), but they will face "*shame and everlasting contempt.*" (See John 5:28-29.) How we respond now to God's offer of salvation through Jesus Christ determines how we will spend eternity.

Unanswered Questions

The book of Daniel concludes in mystery. Daniel asked an angel how it would all turn out. The angel was evasive. Daniel had to be content to live with unanswered questions. But almost as an afterthought, the angel said a bit more. He said that 1,290 days would pass "*from the time that the regular burnt offering is taken away and the abomination that makes desolation is set up*" (12:11). Then he added, "*Blessed is he who waits and arrives at the 1,335 days*" (12:12). The text does not explain, but we can infer that the waiting would be longer than people would think. Patience would be required.

God understood how troubling these visions must have been. Evidently He wanted to comfort Daniel (12:13). So, although Daniel was not told the details of the world's future, he did receive assurance about his personal future. Daniel would rest, and he would stand, faithful to the end.

Personalize this lesson.

When we met Daniel he was a very young man. When we leave him decades later, he is very old. Daniel remained faithful to God throughout his life. No matter how old you are, you can learn from Daniel's example. Are you young? What godly character traits do you need to pray into your life now so that you can remain faithful later? If you are already in your latter years, what do you need to continue to doing (or resume doing) in order to finish strong? Ask God to help you take inventory. What will you need to live strong for Him to the end? Then ask Him to reveal specific action steps to help you follow through.

Small Group Leader's Guide

While *Engaging God's Word* is great for personal study, it is generally even more effective and enjoyable when studied with others. Studying with others provides different perspectives and insights, care, prayer support, and fellowship that studying on your own does not. Depending on your personal circumstances, consider studying with your family or spouse, with a friend, in a Sunday school, with a small group at church, work, or in your neighborhood, or in a mentoring relationship.

In a traditional Community Bible Study class, your study would involve a proven four-step method: personal study, a small group discussion facilitated by a trained leader, a lecture covering the passage of Scripture, and a written commentary about the same passage. *Engaging God's Word* provides two of these four steps with the study questions and commentary. When you study with a group, you add another of these— the group discussion. And if you enjoy teaching, you could even provide a modified form of the fourth, the lecture, which in a small group setting might be better termed a wrap-up talk.

Here are some suggestions to help leaders facilitate a successful group study.

1. Decide how long you would like each group meeting to last. For a very basic study, without teaching, time for fellowship, or group prayer, plan on one hour. If you want to allow for fellowship before the meeting starts, add at least 15 minutes. If you plan to give a short teaching, add 15 or 20 minutes. If you also want time for group prayer, add another 10 or 15 minutes. Depending on the components you include for your group, each session will generally last between one and two hours.

2. Set a regular time and place to meet. Meeting in a church classroom or a conference room at work is fine. Meeting in a home is also a good option, and sometimes more relaxed and comfortable.

3. Publicize the study and/or personally invite people to join you.

4. Begin praying for those who have committed to come. Continue to pray for them individually throughout the course of the study.

5. Make sure everyone has his or her own book at least a week before you meet for the first time.

6. Encourage group members to read the first lesson and do the questions before they come to the group meeting.

7. Prepare your own lesson.

8. Prepare your wrap-up talk, if you plan to give one. Here is a simple process for developing a wrap-up talk:

   a. Divide the passage you are studying into two or three divisions. Jot down the verses for each division and describe the content of each with one complete sentence that answers the question, "What is the passage about?"

   b. Decide on the central idea of your wrap-up talk. The central idea is the life-changing principle found in the passage that you believe God wants to implant in the hearts and minds of your group. The central idea answers the question, "What does God want us to learn from this passage?"

   c. Provide one illustration that would make your central idea clear and meaningful to your group. This could be an illustration from your own life, or a story you've read or heard somewhere else.

   d. Suggest one application that would help your group put the central idea into practice.

   e. Choose an aim for your wrap-up talk. The aim answers the question, "What does God want us to do about it?" It encourages specific change in your group's lives, if they choose to respond to the central idea of the passage. Often it takes the form of a question you will ask your group: "Will you, will I choose to … ?"

9. Show up early to the study so you can arrange the room, set up the refreshments (if you are serving any), and welcome people as they arrive.

10. Whether your meeting includes a fellowship time or not, begin the discussion time promptly each week. People appreciate it when you respect their time. Transition into the discussion with prayer, inviting God to guide the discussion time and minister personally to each person present.

11. Model enthusiasm to the group. Let them know how excited you are about what you are learning—and your eagerness to hear what God is teaching them.

12. As you lead through the questions, encourage everyone to participate, but don't force anyone. If one or two people tend to dominate the discussion, encourage quieter ones to participate by saying something like, "Let's hear from someone who hasn't shared yet." Resist the urge to teach during discussion time. This time is for your group to share what they have been discovering.

13. Try to allow time after the questions have been discussed to talk about the "Apply what you have learned," "Think about" and "Personalize this lesson" sections. Encourage your group members in their efforts to partner with God in allowing Him to transform their lives.

14. Transition into the wrap-up talk, if you are doing one (see number 8).

15. Close in prayer. If you have structured your group to allow time for prayer, invite group members to pray for themselves and one another, especially focusing on the areas of growth they would like to see in their lives as a result of their study. If you have not allowed time for group prayer, you as leader can close this time.

16. Before your group finishes their final lesson, start praying and planning for what your next *Engaging God's Word* study will be.

About Community Bible Study

For almost 40 years Community Bible Study
has taught the Word of God through in-depth,
community-based Bible studies. With nearly 700
classes in the United States as well as classes in
more than 70 countries, Community Bible Study purposes to be an
"every-person's Bible study, available to all."

Classes for men, women, youth, children, and even babies, are all
designed to make members feel loved, cared for, and accepted—
regardless of age, ethnicity, socio-economic status, education, or
church membership. Because Bible study is most effective in one's heart
language, Community Bible Study curriculum has been translated into
more than 50 languages.

Community Bible Study makes every effort to stand in the center of the
mainstream of historic Christianity, concentrating on the essentials of
the Christian faith rather than denominational distinctives. Community
Bible Study respects different theological views, preferring to focus on
helping people to know God through His Word, grow deeper in their
relationships with Jesus, and be transformed into His likeness.

Community Bible Study's focus ... is to glorify God by providing
in-depth Bible studies and curriculum in a Christ-centered, grace-filled,
and philosophically safe environment.

Community Bible Study's passion ... is the transformation of
individuals, families, communities, and generations through the power
of God's Word, making disciples of the Lord Jesus Christ.

Community Bible Study's relationship with local churches ... is one
of support and respect. Community Bible Study classes are composed of
people from many different churches; they are designed to complement
and not compete with the ministry of the local church. Recognizing that
the Lord has chosen the local church as His primary channel of ministry,
Community Bible Study encourages class members to belong to and
actively support their local churches and to be servants and leaders in
their congregations.

Do you want to experience lasting transformation in your life? Are you ready to go deeper in God's Word? There is probably a Community Bible Study near you! Find out by visiting www.findmyclass.org or scan the QR code on this page.

For more information:

Call   800-826-4181

Email   info@communitybiblestudy.org

Web   www.communitybiblestudy.org

Class   www.findmyclass.org

Where will your next Bible study adventure take you?

Engage Bible Studies help you discover the joy and the richness of God's Word and apply it your life.

Check out these titles for your next adventure:

Engaging God's Word: Genesis

Engaging God's Word: Deuteronomy

Engaging God's Word: Joshua & Judges

Engaging God's Word: Ruth & Esther

Engaging God's Word: Daniel

Engaging God's Word: Job

Engaging God's Word: Mark

Engaging God's Word: Luke

Engaging God's Word: Acts

Engaging God's Word: Romans

Engaging God's Word: Galatians

Engaging God's Word: Ephesians

Engaging God's Word: Philippians

Engaging God's Word: Colossians

Engaging God's Word: 1 & 2 Thessalonians

Engaging God's Word: Hebrews

Engaging God's Word: James

Engaging God's Word: 1 & 2 Peter

Engaging God's Word: Revelation

Available at Amazon.com and in fine bookstores.

Visit engagebiblestudies.com